CONTENTS

DIRECTOR'S FOREWORD

Viewing sequentially the very large number of photographic portraits submitted from around the world might produce a numbing effect. What occurs is the reverse. The intensity of the process of viewing – with more than 5,000 actual prints, presented anonymously without any knowledge of the photographer – increases one's responsiveness to minute nuances and critical accents in each portrait. The presentation of an individual or group of people, as chosen by the photographer and translated with great skill into the final portrait, brings the viewing eye to take in, simultaneously, the pose, the setting, the lighting, the occasion and narrative, and then to focus on the character and personality of the individuals who appear in each portrait.

In the most successful portraits this crucial combination produces something compelling that causes us, as viewers, to be held by the image: to look closely and to look again. In our present digital world, with a vast number of images of people endlessly circulating in the media, these photographic portraits stand out because of the skills that create precisely this clarity, this quality of attentiveness.

I was very grateful, as always, to the photographers who submitted 5,340 images to the *Taylor Wessing Photographic Portrait Prize* 2012. Many congratulations go to this year's winners: Jordi Ruiz Cirera, Jennifer Pattison, Spencer Murphy and Alma Haser. I am also grateful to Simon Crocker, Chairman of the John Kobal Foundation, and to Liz Jobey, Trustee, for their collaboration through which a younger photographer is awarded the 2012 John Kobal New Work Award and a commission to make a new portrait from within the world of film.

I should like to thank my fellow judges: Emma Hardy, Lauren Heinz, Glyn Morgan, Sean O'Hagan and Terence Pepper. They were equally discerning and passionate in their choices across the two days, and produced a hugely creative debate to reach the final sixty. Thanks also go to National Portrait Gallery staff, the designers Thomas Manss & Company and the interviewer Richard McClure for all their hard work on the exhibition and the catalogue. I am grateful to The White Wall Company for their expert contribution to the logistical management of the submission and judging process.

My final thanks go to Taylor Wessing and to Tim Eyles, UK Managing Partner. The partnership is hugely appreciated by the Gallery and is developing each year, offering the public in London, and on tour, an outstanding exhibition.

SANDY NAIRNE
DIRECTOR, NATIONAL PORTRAIT GALLERY

SPONSOR'S FOREWORD

This is the fifth year of Taylor Wessing's sponsorship of the *Photographic Portrait Prize*. You might think the thrill of being involved in the Prize would diminish with familiarity, but the reality is that each year the extraordinary variety and quality of the entries creates a renewed sense of excitement.

New and multifarious themes and ideas always emerge in the portraits, which often reflect current events and issues. I am sure it is no coincidence, for example, that portraits of two of Britain's greatest Olympians are among this year's finalists. What links each year though, is the insight that the photographs provide into the human spirit, with portraits of individuals from different cultures and societies capturing something profoundly human that we, the viewers, can relate to. Photography is powerful in its ability to capture an expression or a look in a person's eye that hints at something deeper than what might be apparent superficially. Perhaps that's the reason why this exhibition is so evocative and I would urge anyone reading this to go and see it for themselves.

Taylor Wessing attaches great importance to supporting the arts and, in our firm's culture, to creativity. The *Taylor Wessing Photographic Portrait Prize* in particular correlates with our own values: its encouragement and cultivation of new talent alongside that of established professionals; the wonderful diversity of images that provoke such varied reactions; and the far-reaching, international nature of the competition.

We are fortunate in that working alongside the National Portrait Gallery we have the opportunity to add another dimension to the work we do with our charity partners, this year using photography as a tool of communication and inspiration for a group of children from Kids Company, a wonderful charity that provides practical, emotional and educational support to vulnerable inner-city children.

I hope that you will share our enjoyment of the works in this year's Prize. Among portraits that are enigmatic, tender, shocking, funny or simply beautiful, there is something to inspire everyone. All of us at Taylor Wessing would like to congratulate everyone, including each and every entrant, who has helped to create yet another inspiring exhibition. Our thanks and gratitude also go to the National Portrait Gallery, with whom we look forward to a continuing partnership over the coming years.

TIM EYLES
MANAGING PARTNER, TAYLOR WESSING LLP

TaylorWessing

PHOTOGRAPHY AND SILENCE
SEAN O'HAGAN

The more I look at great photographs, the more I realise what Henri Cartier-Bresson meant when he said: 'The most difficult thing for me is a portrait.' For him, the portrait was a particular kind of quest. When he described the singular nature of that quest, he spoke not about light or composition, but about stillness and quiet. 'In a portrait,' he explained, 'I am looking for the silence in somebody.'

The first photograph that struck me with the full force of its silence was Josef Koudelka's snatched portrait of a young man in handcuffs on a desolate road on the edge of a village in Slovakia. I came across it while poring over a second-hand copy of Koudelka's *Gypsies* – the first photography book I ever bought. The silence seems to me to begin in the young man's staring eyes and emanate outwards across the whole image, rendering silent everything around it: the crowd of curious onlookers in the background as well as the policemen – and the police dog – standing on that desolate road. Koudelka's snatched portrait is powerful even if you do not know, as I did not know for many years, that the young man in question had just murdered his wife. Perhaps the silence that Koudelka caught emanates from that terrible moment of violence, from an act unwitnessed and unrecorded by his camera.

Not all photographic portraits, of course, possess this kind of power. Even a cursory glance at the sixty images that have made it into the National Portrait Gallery's *Taylor Wessing Photographic Portrait Prize* 2012 exhibition will show how the imposed limits of photographic portraiture can conversely lead to a richness of interpretation and style. Some evince thoughtfulness, others exuberance or reticence, or even the palpable unease of the subject. A formal portrait though, perhaps more than any other kind of photograph, is the result of a collaboration between the individuals on either side of the camera, but the outcome is always uncertain. What's more, a truly great portrait will accrue several layers of meaning – and of deepening silence – as the years go by. 'As time passes by and you look at portraits,' mused an ageing Cartier-Bresson, 'the people come back to you like a silent echo.'

As has been already noted, perhaps most eloquently by the great French thinker, Roland Barthes, every photographic portrait speaks of mortality: the subject's and our own. It freezes time and therefore highlights the inevitability of time's passing. A snapshot can convey this sense of mortality, of transience, just as powerfully as a carefully posed portrait, and sometimes more so. A found photograph of a stranger from another time can awaken some vague longing within us that we did not know we had and maybe cannot fully articulate. More mysteriously still, a single detail in a photograph – a frayed cuff, an object in the background, a familiar look – can, in Barthes' words, 'prick' and 'bruise' the viewer with a strange unsettling intensity of emotion.

A photographic portrait is a record of an irretrievable moment in time, a too-real trace of someone already gone – a few days ago, a year ago, a lifetime ago. An echo of that elusive silence that Cartier-Bresson spoke of, sought and so often captured.

THE PRIZES

**TAYLOR WESSING PHOTOGRAPHIC
PORTRAIT PRIZE**

The *Taylor Wessing Photographic Portrait
Prize* is open to photographers from
around the world aged eighteen or over.

The first prize winner is
Jordi Ruiz Cirera, who receives £12,000.

The second prize winner is
Jennifer Pattison, who receives £3,000.

The third prize winner is
Spencer Murphy, who receives £2,000.

The fourth prize winner is
Alma Haser, who receives £1,000.

**THE JOHN KOBAL NEW
WORK AWARD**

The John Kobal New Work Award is
awarded to a photographer under the
age of thirty selected for the exhibition.
The winning photographer receives a cash
prize of £4,000 to include undertaking a
commission from the Gallery to photograph
a sitter connected with the UK film industry.

The winner is Matthew Niederhauser.

If you would like to join the mailing
list to receive an entry form for next
year's *Photographic Portrait Prize*,
please register your interest online
at: www.npg.org.uk/photoprize
or send your full contact details to:

Photographic Portrait Prize 2013
Marketing Department
National Portrait Gallery
St Martin's Place
London WC2H 0HE

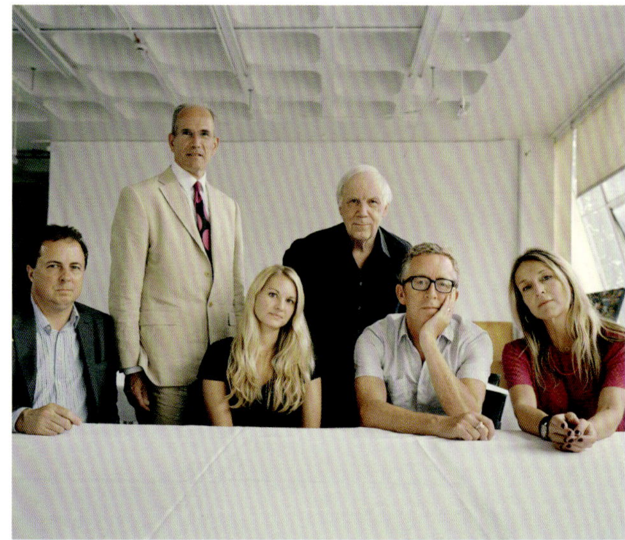

PHOTOGRAPH BY EMMA HARDY, 15 AUGUST 2012

THE JUDGES, LEFT TO RIGHT: GLYN MORGAN,
SANDY NAIRNE, LAUREN HEINZ, TERENCE PEPPER,
SEAN O'HAGAN, EMMA HARDY.

THE JUDGES

CHAIR: SANDY NAIRNE
DIRECTOR, NATIONAL PORTRAIT GALLERY
The startling character of humans is brought into the closest consideration through the best photographic portraits. Whatever the style of the photograph – from studio work to documentary – the final sixty choices for the *Taylor Wessing Photographic Portrait Prize* 2012 represent a vibrant world conveyed to us through the visual skills of each photographer. I offer, as always, my huge thanks to all the photographers who submitted their work and to the close attention given by the judges across the two days.

EMMA HARDY
PHOTOGRAPHER
Whether carefully planned or the result of a chance encounter, if a photographic portrait demands attention from a viewer – by asking a question, telling a story or revealing subjects in frank, unexpected or beautiful detail – it has achieved something. As a photographer I know how challenging it is to collect people in front of a camera so that an instant can reflect something meaningful. Looking at thousands of photographs intensely over two days, I realised more than ever that there is no formula for a successful portrait. It's an indefinable, often complex, alchemy. And so it is with genuine admiration that I see this collection of sixty accomplished portraits as split seconds where everything fell into place; elevating the subject and enriching the viewer, perhaps leaving them changed a little.

LAUREN HEINZ
DIRECTOR, FOTO8
The two days spent judging this year's *Taylor Wessing Photographic Portrait Prize* was an intense and compelling experience. To be involved in an award that places such value on the actual physicality of photographic prints is sadly very rare, and the judging process was made all the more dynamic for it. The quality of work was consistently high, which made choosing the final sixty seem almost impossible and, unfortunately, we had to lose some great photographs. In the end, however, we have a selection of some exceptionally deserving photography, one that reflects more traditional skills as well as bold attempts at creating unique photographic portraiture.

GLYN MORGAN
PARTNER, TAYLOR WESSING LLP
It was a great privilege to take part in the process of selecting the winners of the *Taylor Wessing Photographic Portrait Prize* 2012 and the photographs to be included in the exhibition. The overall standard of entries was very strong and included a tremendous variety of approaches to portraiture. The degree of care and attention that went into the judging process was very high and I learned a great deal from the views and opinions of my fellow judges. Going through all the photographs, I was impressed with the many different ways in which the photographers were able to instil a feeling of sympathy with the subjects – turning what would otherwise simply be a photographic image into a portrait of someone with whom you feel a genuine connection.

SEAN O'HAGAN
WRITER ON PHOTOGRAPHY, THE *OBSERVER* AND THE *GUARDIAN*
The judging process was demanding, exhausting, rewarding and, as it neared its conclusion, emotionally charged in a way I had not expected. The sheer amount of images was daunting initially, but a rhythm emerged, and each of us grew more confident in voicing our opinions. Over 5,000 images became six hundred. Six hundred became one hundred. One hundred became sixty. We each had to accept that certain portraits we liked, even loved, were not going to make it into the final selection for the exhibition. It was tough. There was debate, disagreement, much sighing and shaking of heads, and a lot of painful goodbyes. (Was there sulking? Almost.) For me, that penultimate stage, in which a hundred portraits were whittled down to sixty, was tougher and more emotionally draining than the selection of the final four. Of those four, we all had a favourite but they couldn't all be winners. Then again, making the shortlist is a feat in itself. As is being in a show in the National Portrait Gallery.

TERENCE PEPPER
CURATOR OF PHOTOGRAPHS, NATIONAL PORTRAIT GALLERY
For the 2012 Prize we received yet again a fascinating mix of very high-quality entries, ranging from six-picture portfolios to carefully selected individual photographs. As in previous years the judges reached a consensus on a number of images, but, as ever, each of us spoke out passionately in favour of a particular work. Selection is based on the quality of the photographs alone – the identity of the photographers is only revealed to us later. Two days of judging makes for a very intense period and, in retrospect, provides a fascinating overview of the subjects that move and stimulate many talented photographers who have been inspired to share their work with us.

FIRST PRIZE
JORDI RUIZ CIRERA

Awarded first place in the 2012 *Taylor Wessing Photographic Portrait Prize*, Jordi Ruiz Cirera took his winning image while documenting members of a Mennonite community in the Bolivian lowlands. The Spanish photographer travelled to South America on two occasions, gradually winning the trust of the residents of several colonies located south of Santa Cruz.

More than 50,000 Mennonites live in Bolivia, descendants of Christian Anabaptists who left Germany in the sixteenth century. Famously reclusive, the pacifist sect still speaks Low German and their society prohibits the use of cars and electricity.

'It's a very humble existence,' says Ruiz Cirera. 'They live as their ancestors did, in small, conservative communities devoted to God and sustained by hard work in the fields. Mennonite society is very patriarchal and gender roles are strict.'

Since some Mennonites consider photographs to be a form of graven image, Ruiz Cirera struggled to break down their aversion to the lens. 'It was a really difficult project,' he recalls. 'They were willing to host me in their homes, but they weren't initially willing to be pictured. In some cases, it is forbidden. I stayed there for a month, living with different families, then returned a year later. That's when most of my pictures were taken.'

The Mennonites' uneasy relationship with the camera is reflected in the portrait of twenty-six-year-old Margarita Teichroeb, pictured at the home she shares with her mother and sister. Asking Margarita to pose seated at the kitchen table, Ruiz Cirera took the portrait with a digital 35mm Canon 5D mkII, using only available light.

'I wanted Margarita to look at the camera, but that was a problem for her, and I guess that's why she is partially covering her face. She seems to be afraid of the photographer, unwilling to expose herself to our gaze. Her awkward expression says a lot about the tradition, isolation and lifestyle of this community.'

Mennonite settlements have previously been documented by Magnum photojournalist Larry Towell, and the renowned photo agency's pioneering images have been a profound influence on Ruiz Cirera, who graduated in design in his native Barcelona before moving to the UK in 2011 to gain an MA in Photojournalism and Documentary Photography at the London College of Communication.

His subjects include displaced migrant workers living in refugee camps following the Libyan conflict, and Palestinian children attending the ground-breaking Freedom Theatre in the West Bank. His next project will focus on the proliferation of genetically modified crops in Paraguay, where environmental groups claim chemical poisoning has led to the deaths of local people.

'I'm quite a traditional reportage photographer. However, I do like to think about different ways to tackle a story, like using portraiture to document a lifestyle,' he says. 'I'm attracted by photography that shows the variety of the world, whether picturing the life of small communities or portraying social issues. I'd be happy if my work is able to tell stories that are important to me, and I still believe that photography can move people to act or to get to know a situation. At least that's how I'd like it to be.'
INTERVIEW BY RICHARD MCCLURE

TaylorWessing

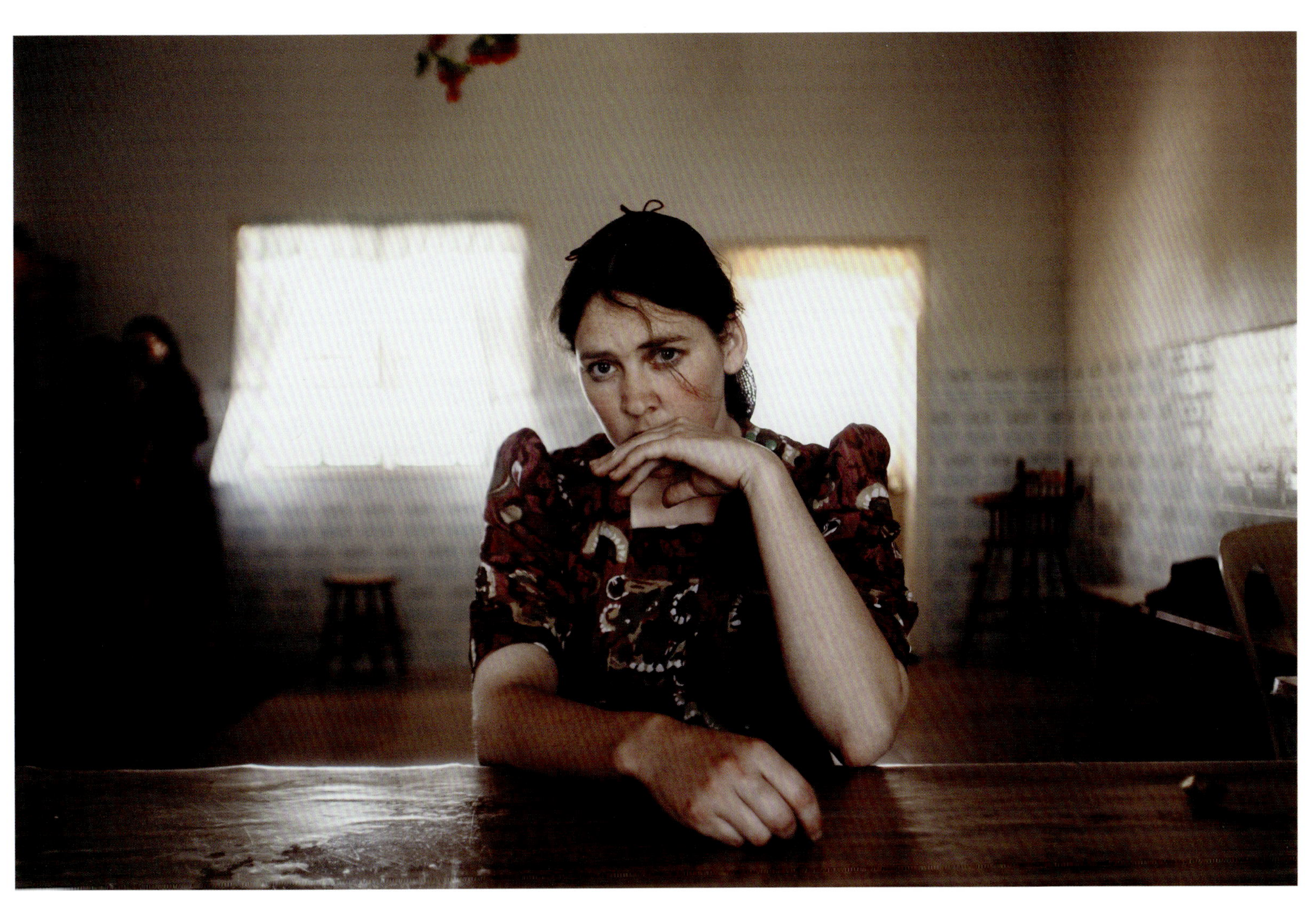

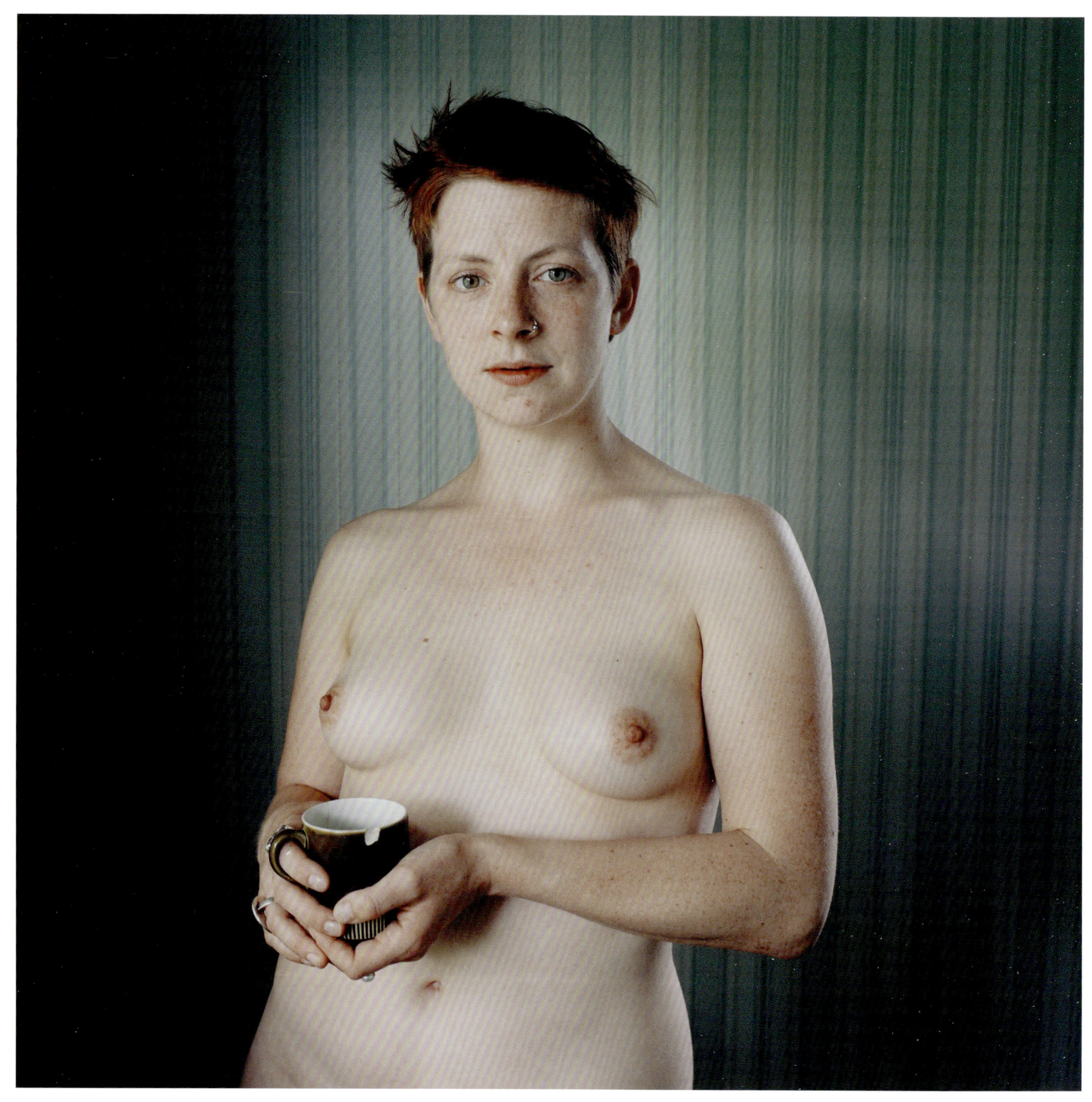

JENNIFER PATTISON
LYNNE, BRIGHTON
MAY 2012

SECOND PRIZE
JENNIFER PATTISON

After leaving the London College of Printing with a degree in Photography in 2000, Jennifer Pattison worked for several years as a photographer's agent and later as a producer, providing support for some of the industry's biggest names on high-profile commissions for the likes of French *Vogue*, Adidas and Honda.

Wishing to 'reconnect with photography creatively' she began an internship in the photography department at the Victoria & Albert Museum in 2006 before realising that her true ambition was to take her own pictures.

'Moving to the V&A reignited my love of story-telling through imagery and encouraged me to get behind the camera full time,' she says. 'Increasingly, I realised that I wanted to bring my own ideas to life. Ever since childhood I have enjoyed the process of taking pictures. By pressing my nose against the back of the camera and looking into the view finder suddenly the everyday becomes elevated.'

Born in Hertfordshire in 1978, Pattison believes that her career as a producer was time well spent, providing insight into the world of commercial photography. 'As a successful producer, with access to world-class photographers, people like David Sims, I was able to watch and learn from some of the best. It also showed me that there is a lot of mediocre image-making, and that to take outstanding pictures you have to stick to your guns. Make the work that excites you, and in turn this will excite others.'

Her entry, *Lynne, Brighton*, comes from an ongoing project that Pattison hopes to complete and exhibit at a London gallery next year. A combination of naked portraits and landscapes, the series is intended to depict the shift in consciousness that occurs when a sitter poses without clothes. 'During the slow process of making these portraits, there is a moment in the quiet where they become unaware that they are naked,' she observes. 'I capture them as they drift to another place.'

The portrait was taken in the empty bedroom of a derelict house in Brighton where her friend Lynne had been living, days before it was demolished. Pattison used a medium-format camera, a Hasselblad 503CW with an 80mm lens, working with daylight and a reflector, and limited herself to three rolls of film. 'The knowledge that there is expensive film running through my camera and I am limited to thirty-six frames forces me to focus and work in a considered way,' she says.

'I don't like to suggest poses. I want to create an honest, frank portrait, which shows the sitter's character. This only comes through in the image if you allow the sitter to arrive at a place where they are comfortable.

'Lynne had set aside the whole day and I had plenty of time so we were both relaxed and unhurried. The house was empty and silent, which influenced our mood. Lynne made coffee and we ate strawberries as the sunshine warmed the room. This all contributed to creating a calm atmosphere. Lynne had seen my work, which gave her confidence that we would get a good result. She trusted me, and I think you can see this in the image.'

INTERVIEW BY RICHARD MCCLURE

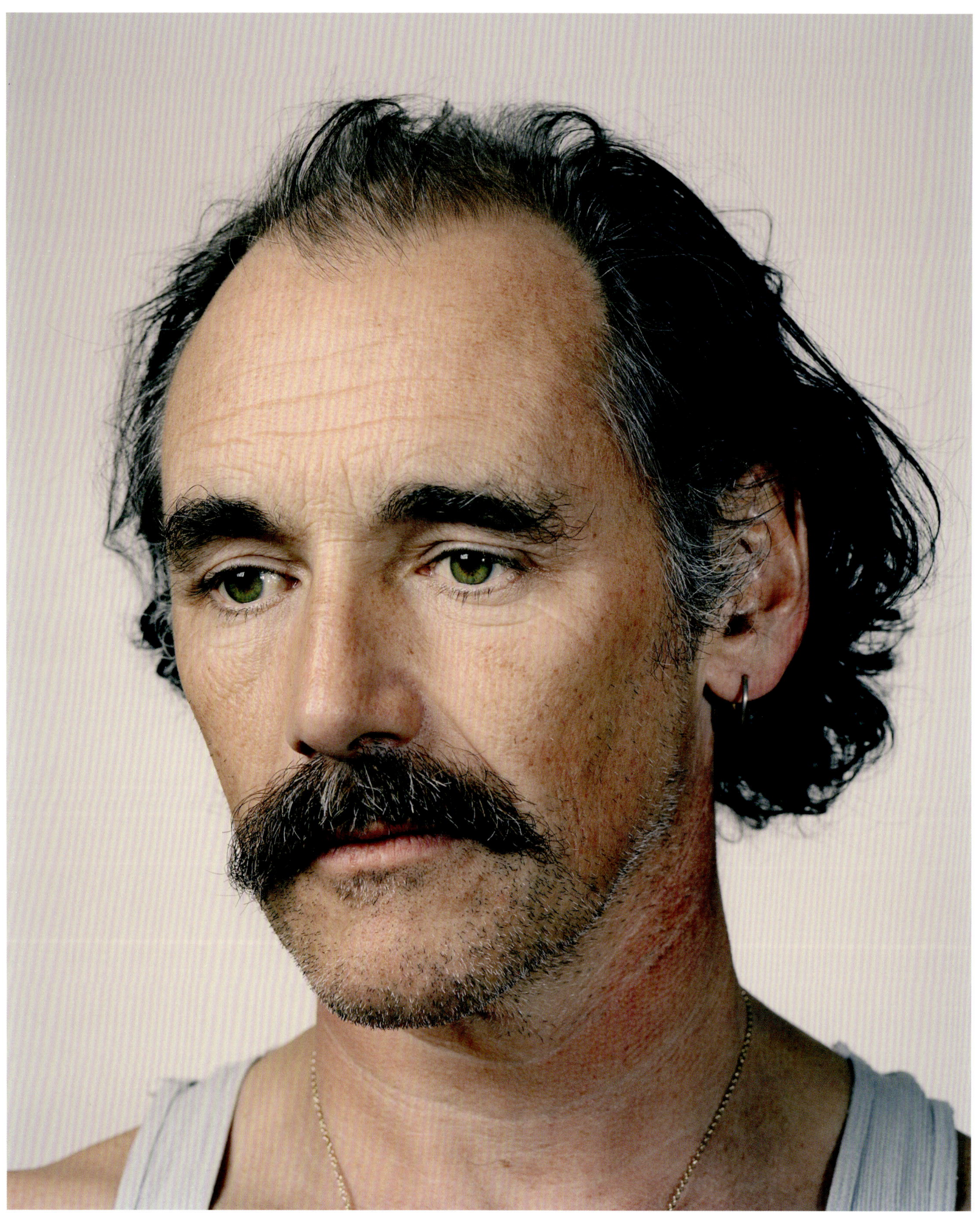

THIRD PRIZE
SPENCER MURPHY

Spencer Murphy's picture of the award-winning actor Mark Rylance is his fifth piece to be selected for exhibition at the National Portrait Gallery in five consecutive years, a feat no other photographer has matched.

As one of Britain's busiest editorial photographers, he works regularly for a number of publications, including the *Guardian Weekend* magazine, for which his recent commissions include portraits of the Archbishop of Canterbury Rowan Williams and former London mayor Ken Livingstone. His portrait of Rylance was commissioned for the cover of the *Sunday Telegraph* magazine as the actor returned to the Globe Theatre to appear in *Richard III* and *Twelfth Night* in the summer of 2012.

While Murphy was aware of Rylance's acclaimed stage performance as Johnny 'Rooster' Byron in Jez Butterworth's *Jerusalem*, he admits to having known 'fairly little' about the actor before the shoot. He believes, however, that familiarity is 'not massively important' in producing a compelling portrait.

'For me, it's a response to someone; perhaps knowing them too well could even cloud how you react to the experience,' he explains. 'Generally, I am a very quiet director. I'll give the sitter an idea of what we are aiming for and then add a few small directions until I see something. I like to work with subtleties of expression – that moment when the guard drops and the mind wanders somewhere.

'It's very much a collaboration, and Mark was great to work with. I usually find actors are; they feel at ease in front of the camera and have a greater understanding of how to channel a feeling or emotion. Apart from that, Mark's features were just a gift. It's a lot about his eyes – there's something genuine and relatable. The closeness and stillness of the picture allows us real access and empathy.'

Setting up in a rehearsal room at the Globe, Murphy shot a variety of set-ups over the course of an hour, using Profoto flash and an RZ pro2 medium-format film camera, the equipment he uses for the majority of his work. 'I like the quality of film more than digital and I prefer the process of not seeing exactly what you are getting other than a few Polaroids as a guide. It makes me push a little more to ensure I've got the picture.'

Murphy was born in 1978 and grew up in rural Kent where the discovery of his mother's back issues of *Life* and *National Geographic* magazines sparked an early enthusiasm for photography. He now lives in London, dividing his time between photographic commissions and creating his own artworks, both portraits and landscapes, that explore notions of existence and man's relationship with nature.

'It can be a struggle to combine commercial and personal work, but I try where possible to bring the same sensibility to both,' he says. 'It is important to keep up the personal projects because it feeds and informs the commercial side and keeps things fresh. I'm still trying to find that balance, but I'm just happy if I can wake up in the morning and take pictures.'
INTERVIEW BY RICHARD MCCLURE

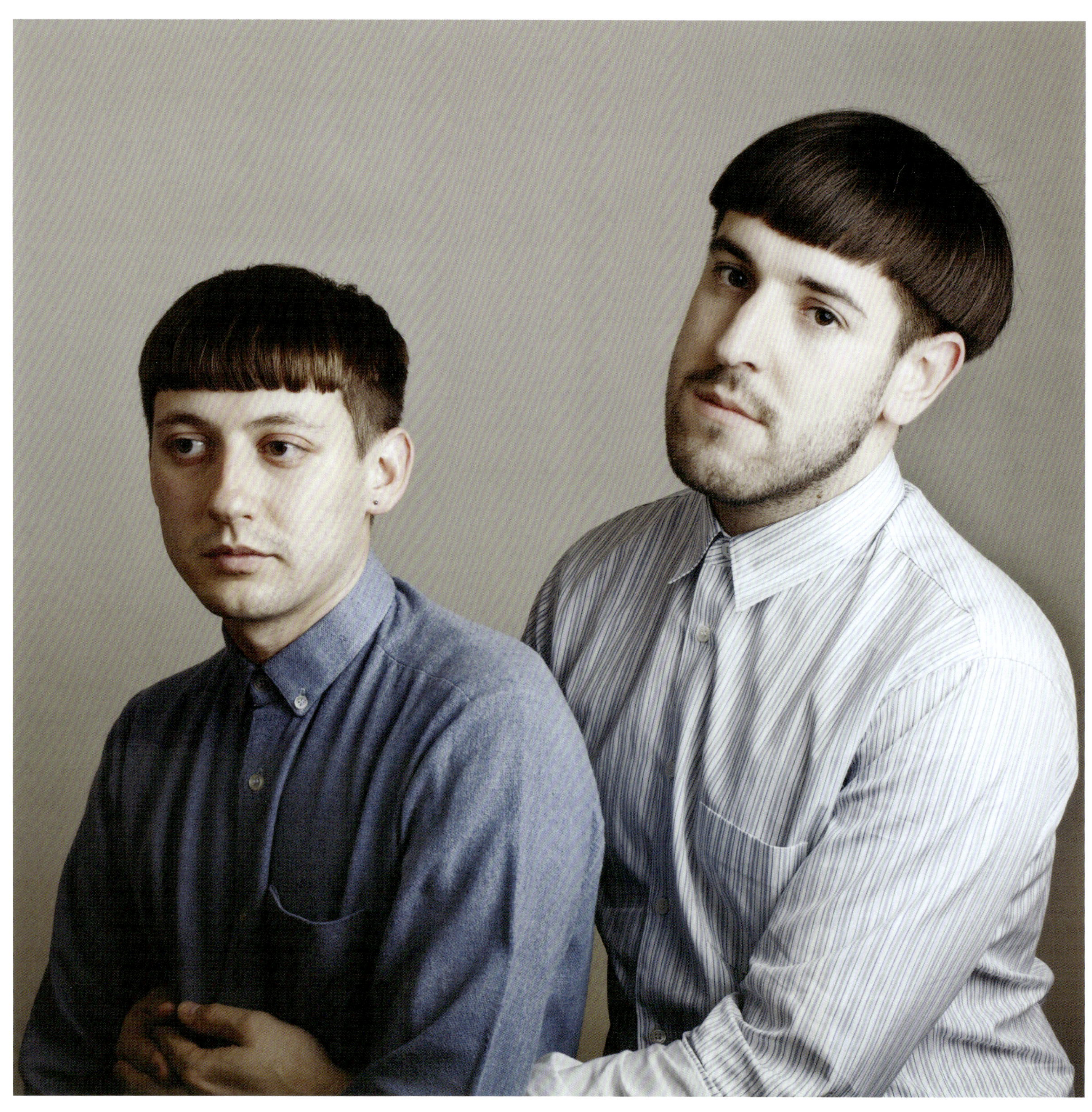

ALMA HASER
THE VENTRILOQUIST
MAY 2012

FOURTH PRIZE
ALMA HASER

Growing up in a squat in an abandoned match factory in Germany, Alma Haser credits her parents with nurturing her interest in photography. She received her first camera, a box Brownie, on her eighth birthday and started by taking self-portraits, surrounded by her dolls, and developing the pictures in her mother's darkroom.

'My life has always been very creative; both my parents are artists, so it was hard not to follow in their footsteps,' she says. 'My mother picked up photography with great vigour, and often had me posing, so my interest grew. I'm quite dyslexic and only started reading when I was eleven, so I tend to use photography as a tool to express how I see things. I always have crazy ideas and my imagination often runs wild.'

Graduating from Nottingham Trent University in 2010 with a degree in Photography as Art Practice, Haser moved to London earlier this year to establish herself as an artist/photographer. Seeking to connect with the viewer by 'telling stories and working with narratives', she has produced a number of inventive and playful series that include *Stateless*, which employs images of stuffed birds as a metaphor for freedom and identity, and *Cosmic Surgery*, a set of surreal portraits in which her sitters' faces are obscured by origami shapes.

Haser met the subjects of her *Taylor Wessing Photographic Portrait Prize* entry, best friends Luke and James, at a party, and initially thought they would make good models for *Cosmic Surgery*. Instead, while photographing the pair in the living room of her south London home, she decided that the dynamic of the picture was strong enough to hold its own as an independent image.

'Luke and James arrived almost an hour late in a whirlwind of banter,' she recalls. 'In a room together they became like brothers, joking and playing around. I tried to do separate portraits, but found it almost impossible to get them to focus. I really liked their closeness and wanted to portray that, exaggerating their amazing size difference by making Luke slouch and James sit bolt upright. With their identical haircuts they looked like twins.'

Haser has explained that the title, *The Ventriloquist*, is designed to help the viewer make up his or her own story about what is going on. 'The bond that Luke and James have with each other is like a connection between them that is stronger than just friendship. Their likeness in style is almost mimicry. Ultimately, I wanted to turn their verbal banter into a visual image.'

Haser shot the portrait with studio lights, tripod and digital camera, printing out the image on her home printer then re-photographing the portrait. 'The thin paper I print onto takes a lot of the saturation out of the colours, which I really like, because it gives the portrait a soft and muted appearance,' she explains.

'But each project demands a different way of working. I'm only twenty-three. I enjoy making work, but don't tend to have any specific themes. I am at the stage in my life where I'm still figuring out all that.'
INTERVIEW BY RICHARD MCCLURE

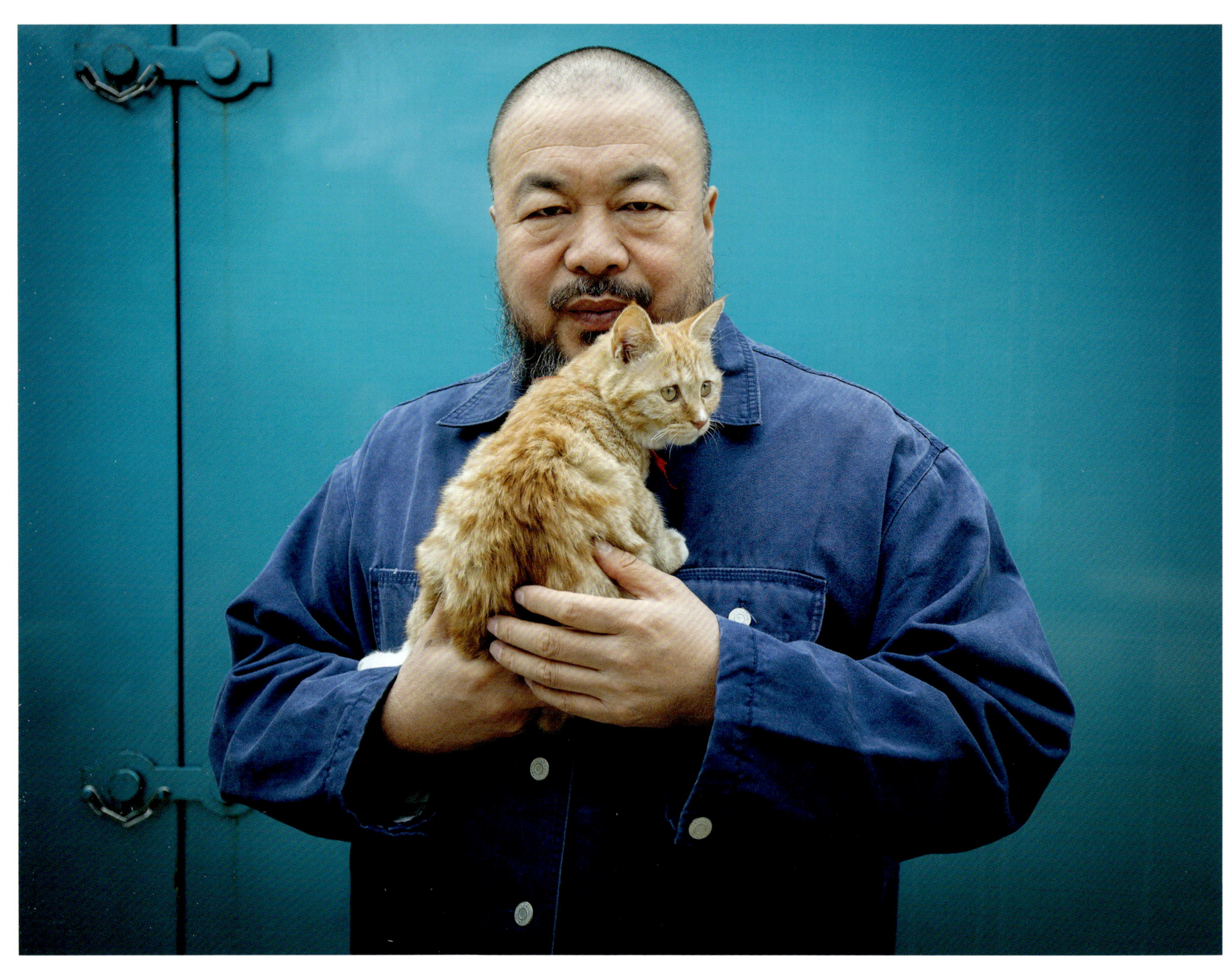

JOHN KOBAL NEW WORK AWARD
MATTHEW NIEDERHAUSER

Matthew Niederhauser's fascination with China was forged during his high-school studies in Mandarin, and the American photographer now lives in Beijing, where he documents aspects of Chinese life for a range of publications including the *New Yorker* and *Time*.

His first monograph, *Sound Kapital*, shed light on Beijing's underground music scene through portraiture and concert photography, while current projects investigate 'megablock' urban development and emerging consumer trends across the country.

'China is my great visual inspiration; there is so much to capture,' says thirty-year-old Niederhauser. 'I am consistently overwhelmed by the country's rate of change and sheer immensity. As of yet, the government has never interfered with my work, but there are definitely lines you know not to cross if you wish to continue there.'

Artist and political activist Ai Weiwei, the subject of Niederhauser's entry, has crossed those lines on many occasions. At the time the portrait was taken, as a commission for *Foreign Policy* magazine, Ai was being held under virtual house arrest and forbidden to leave China following his three-month detention a year earlier.

Aware of his sitter's high repute within artistic and political circles, Niederhauser admits to feeling a 'little pressure' before the shoot at Ai's studio complex in northeast Beijing. 'But working with him ended up being a breeze,' he recalls. 'The only oddity was that Ai enjoys taking his own photographs of photographers as they take his portrait. A number of my shots are of him with his iPhone trained on me. It became a game of cat and mouse as we took pictures of each other. Apparently, he has quite a collection of photographs of photographers taking his portrait.'

For the hour-long shoot, Niederhauser alternated between his Canon 5D Mark II and a Hasselblad, working without artificial lighting in the belief that it 'distracts the sitter and often kills any mood the environment might offer'. The portrait was among the last he took. Wanting to capture Ai with one of the many cats that hang around his compound, Niederhauser persuaded him to pose with a ginger stray, its colouring setting off the teal-blue gates of the studio. 'There was a tense moment when I didn't think the cat was going to cooperate, but it finally glanced back, allowing me to get a few frames with everything melding together.'

As the recipient of the John Kobal New Work Award, given to a photographer under the age of thirty selected for the exhibition, Niederhauser receives a cash prize of £4,000 and a commission from the National Portrait Gallery to photograph a sitter connected with the UK film industry. Niederhauser, who combines photography with his own film and video projects, has suggested that Guy Ritchie, Daniel Day-Lewis or Ridley Scott would all be intriguing possibilities. 'Starting out, I would be torn between filming and photographing, but eventually I found greater balance,' he says. 'Sometimes the image is more powerful and sometimes the video. They are totally interrelated, but I believe photographic imagery plays quite uniquely upon the human mind. It resonates more closely with lived experience, and in that sense it can touch the viewer more deeply.'

INTERVIEW BY RICHARD MCCLURE

THE TAYLOR WESSING
PHOTOGRAPHIC
PORTRAIT
PRIZE
EXHIBITORS

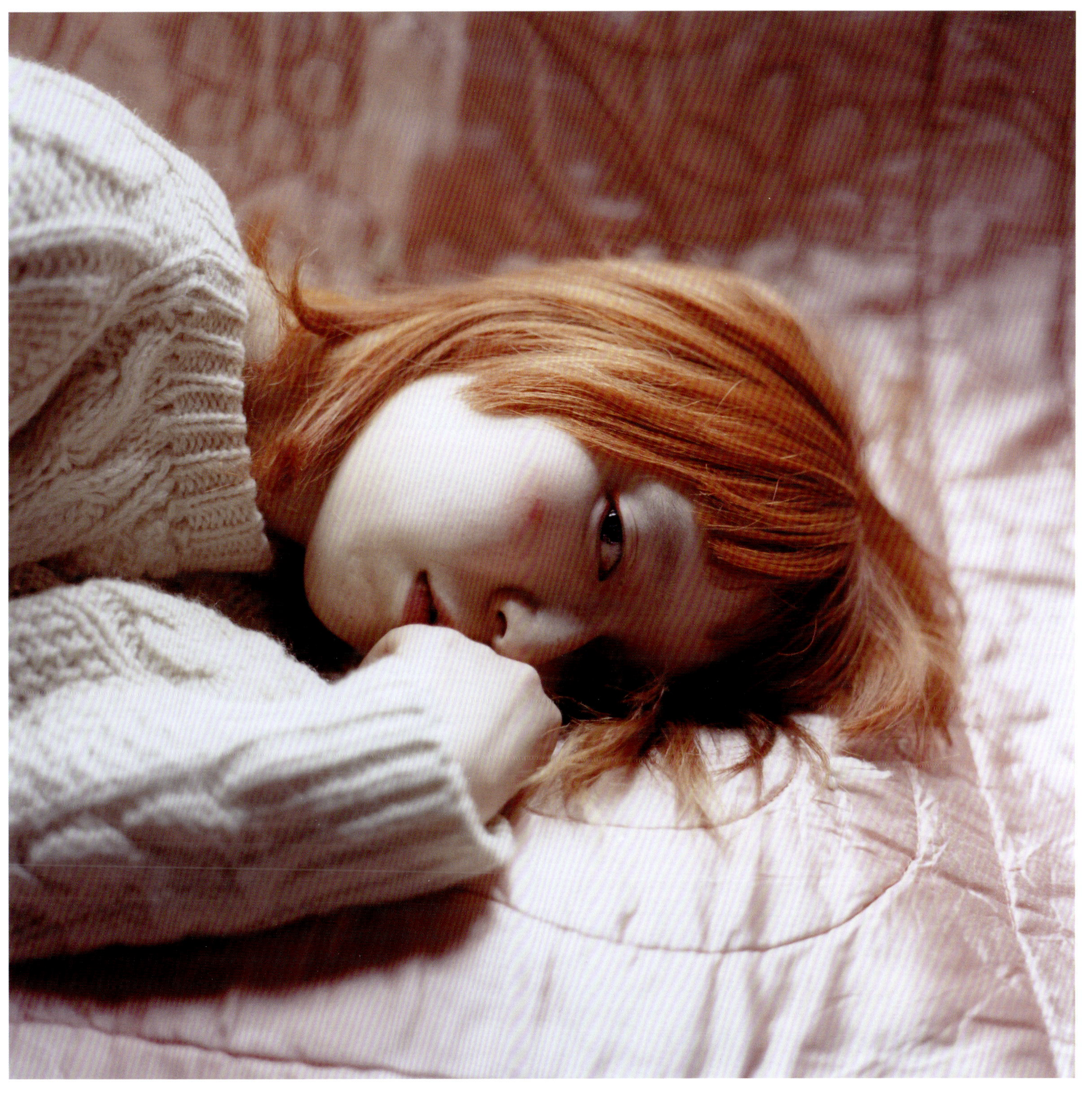

ANNIE COLLINGE
MARI, BROOKLYN
FEBRUARY 2012

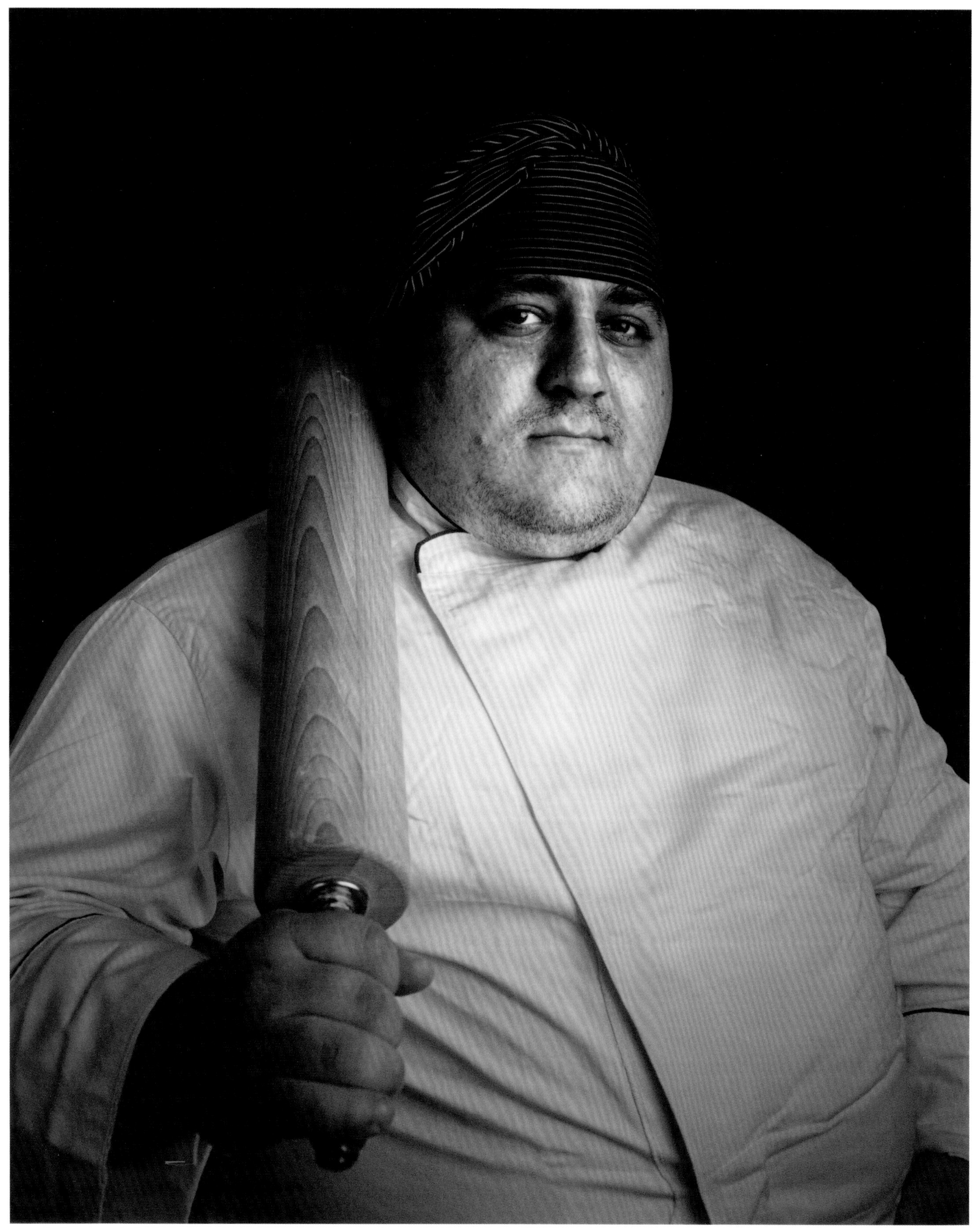

JASON PIERCE-WILLIAMS
PASTRY CHEF
FROM THE SERIES *LOCALS*
MAY 2012

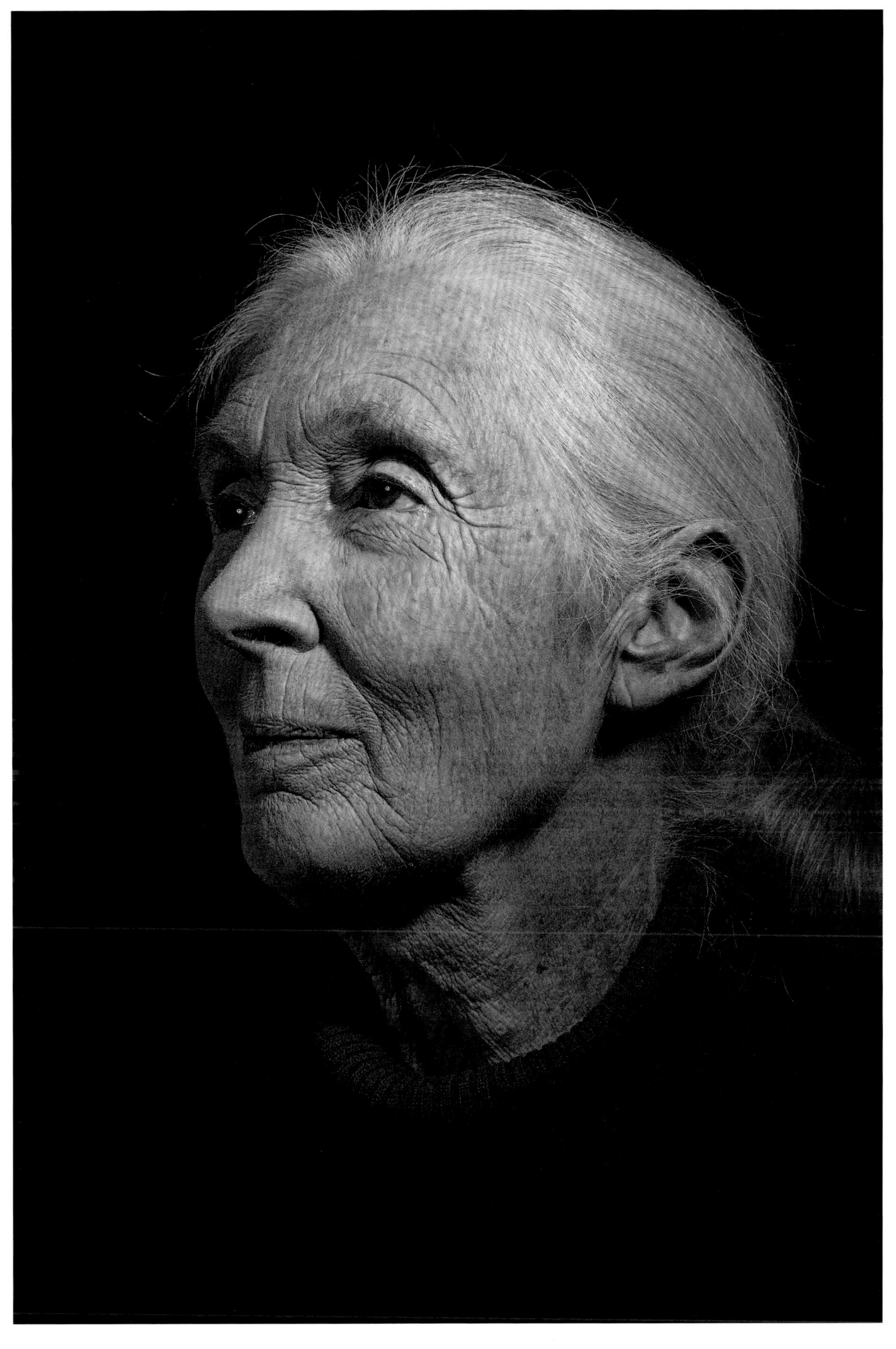

SAM FAULKNER
JANE GOODALL
MAY 2012

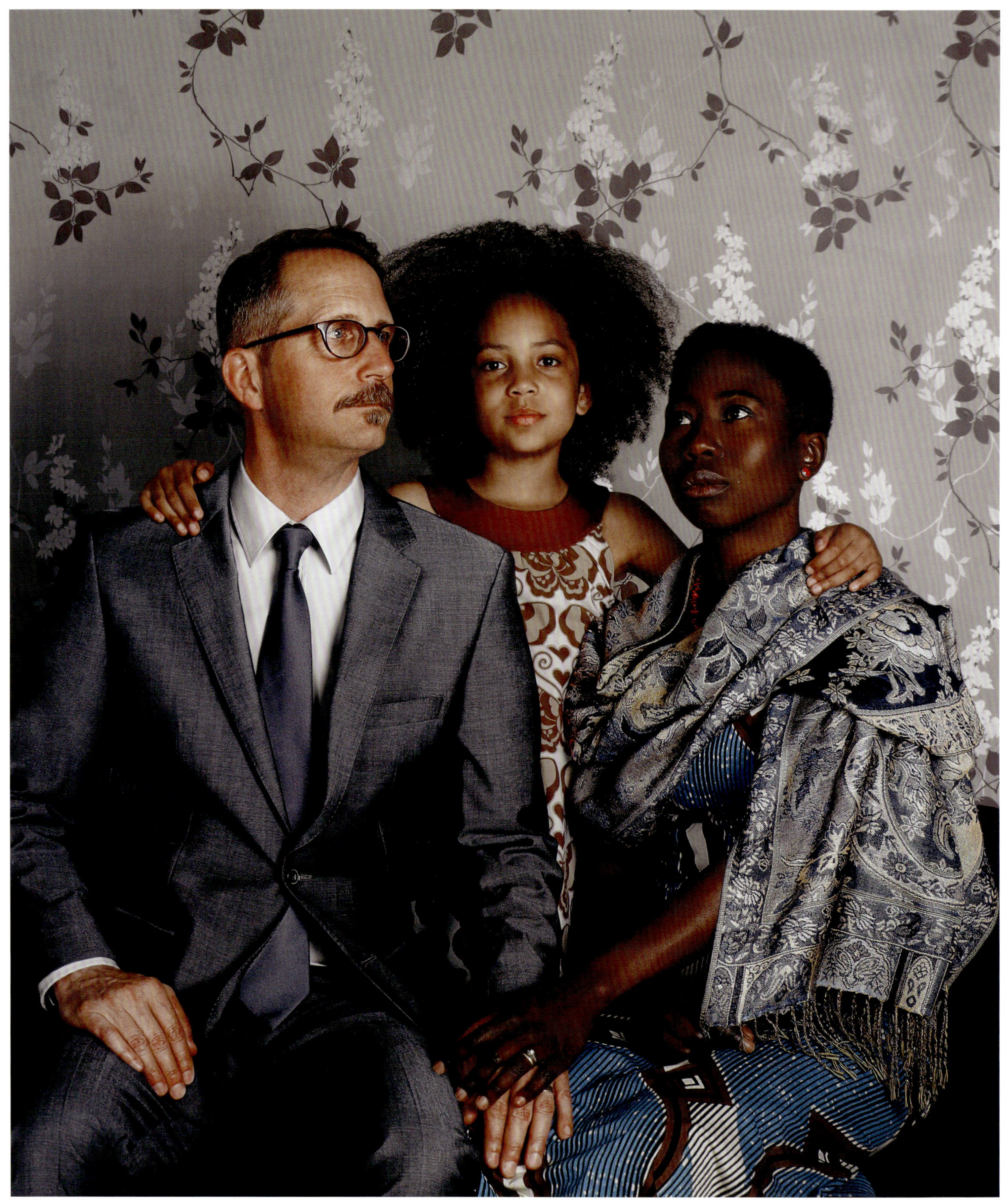

GANDEE VASAN

DAVITA, SITALI AND PAUL
JULY 2012

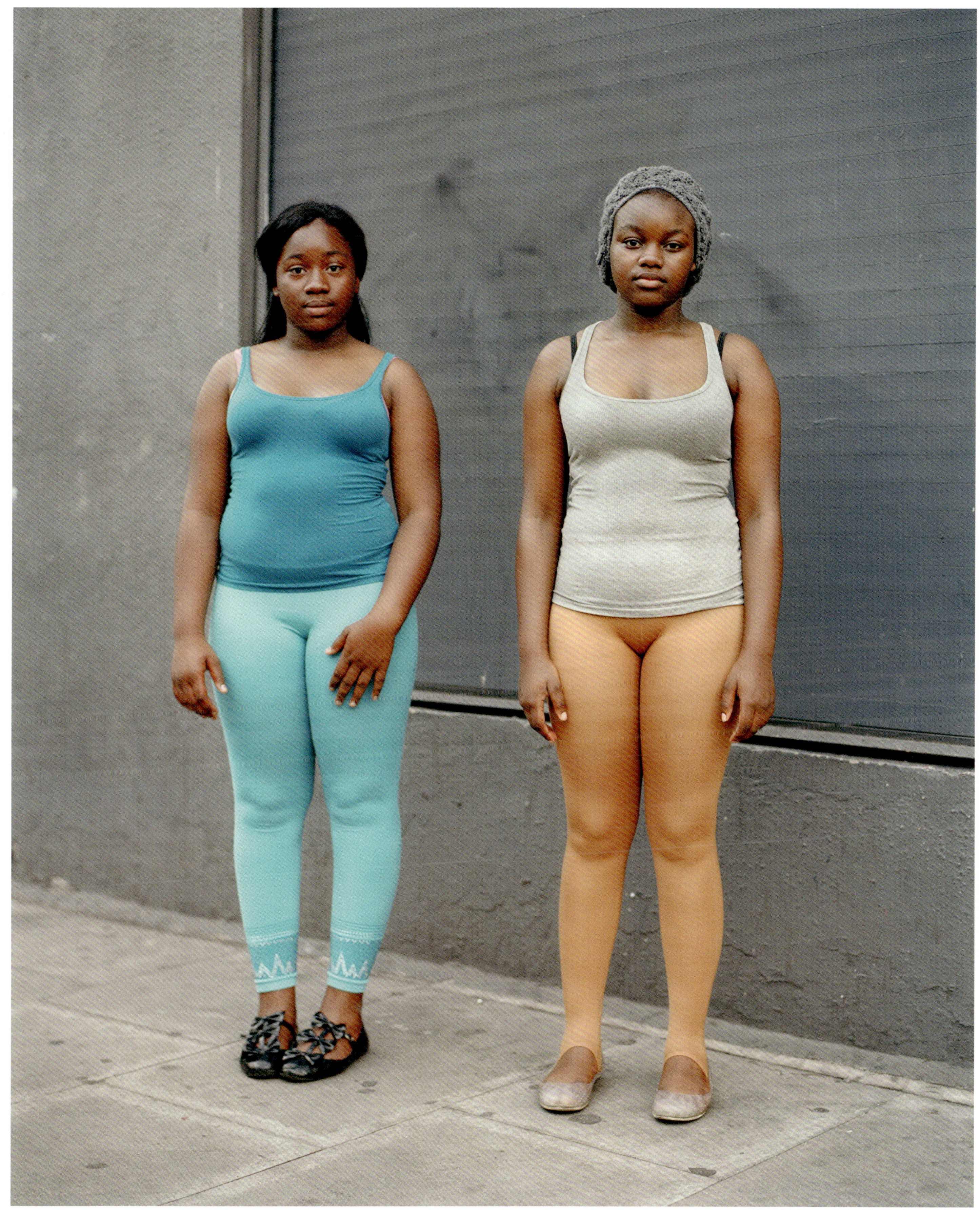

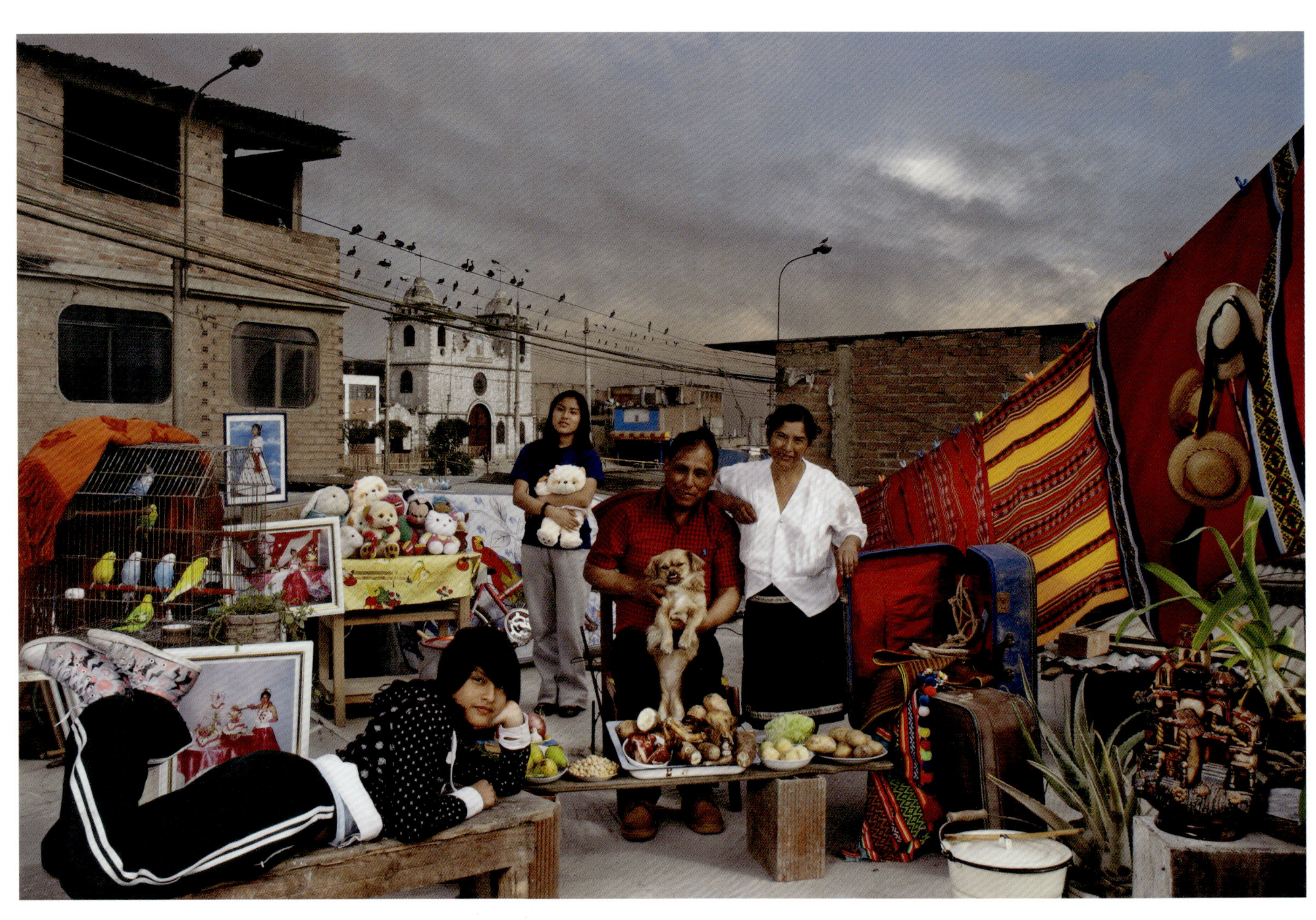

PROYECTO MIRAME
MELQUIADINA AND HER FAMILY
FROM THE SERIES *MIRAME – LIMA*
OCTOBER 2011

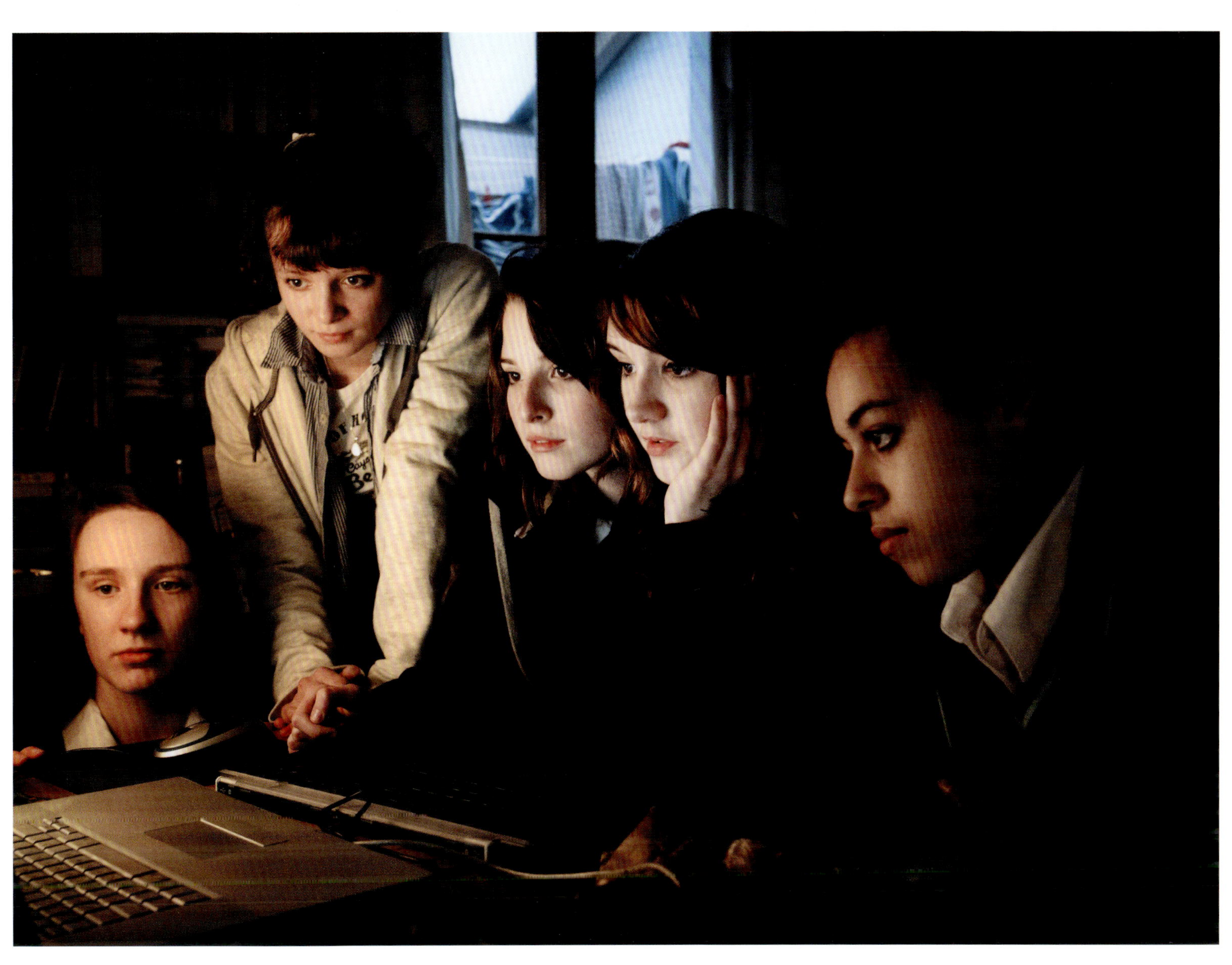

JAMES RUSSELL CANT
HEATHER AND HER FRIENDS
JANUARY 2011

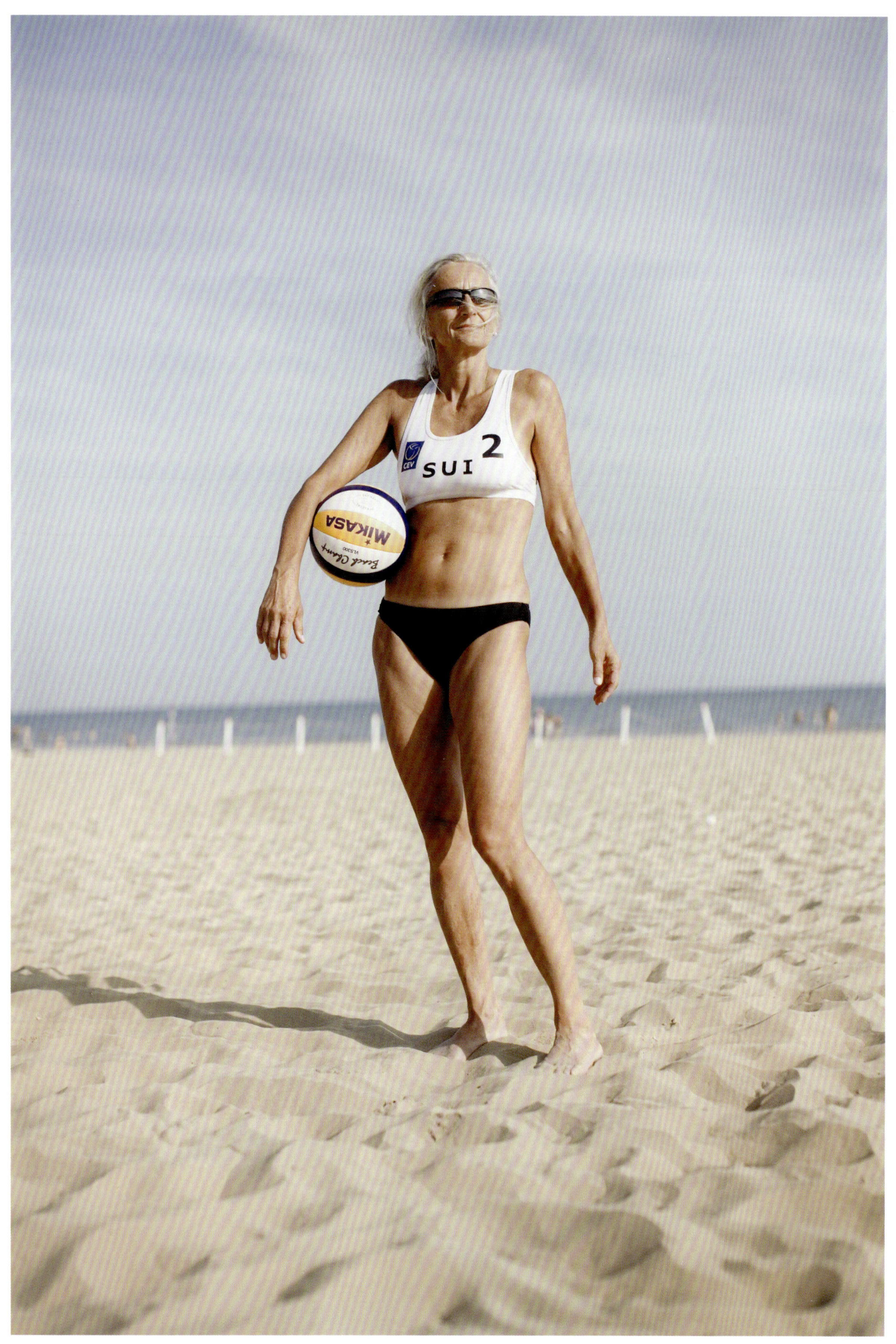

THOMAS BUTLER
HELENA MÜLLER 53 – BEACH VOLLEYBALL
SEPTEMBER 2011

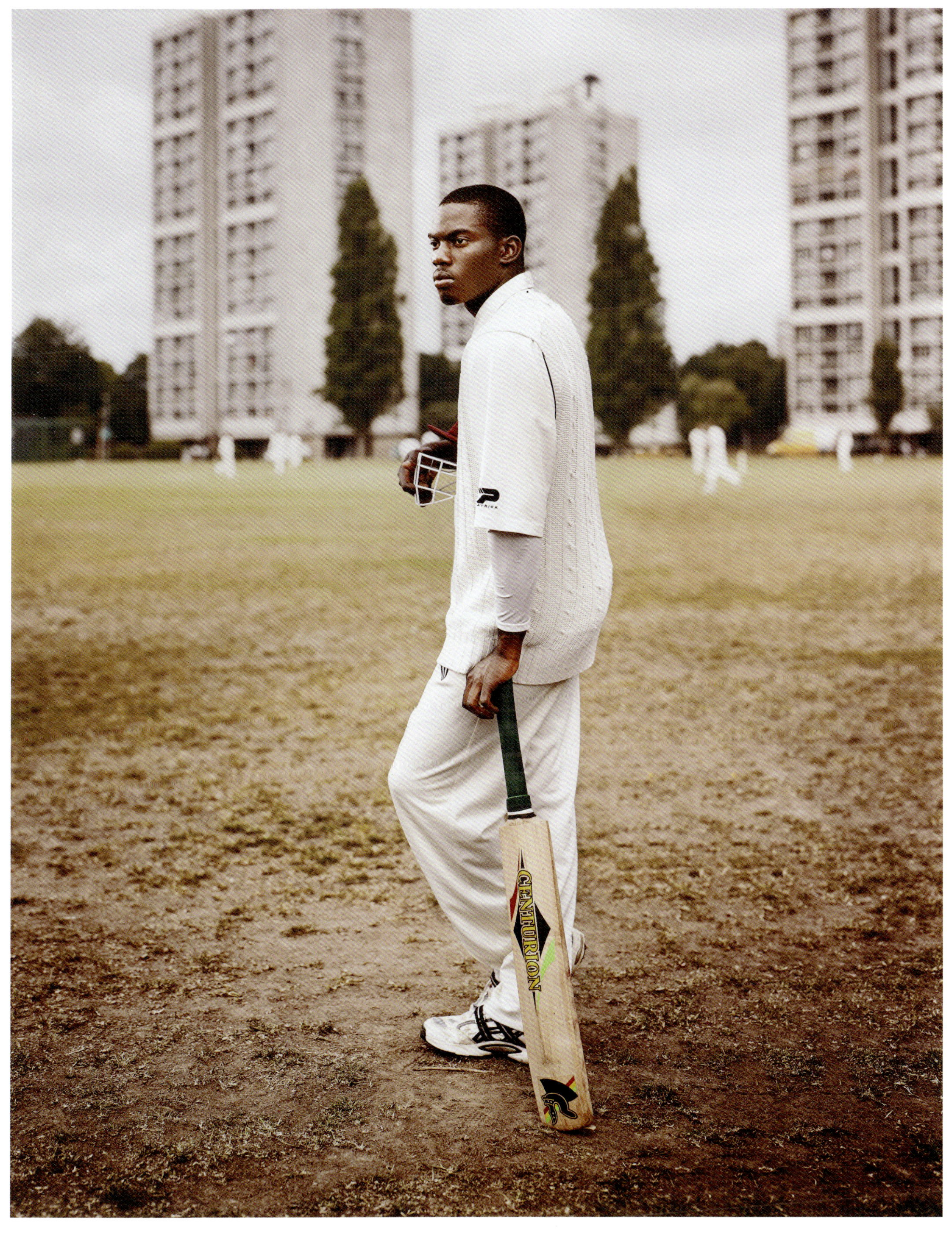

DYLAN COLLARD
12TH MAN: JORDAN
FROM THE SERIES *12TH MAN: SPORT CITY LONDON*
SEPTEMBER 2011

25

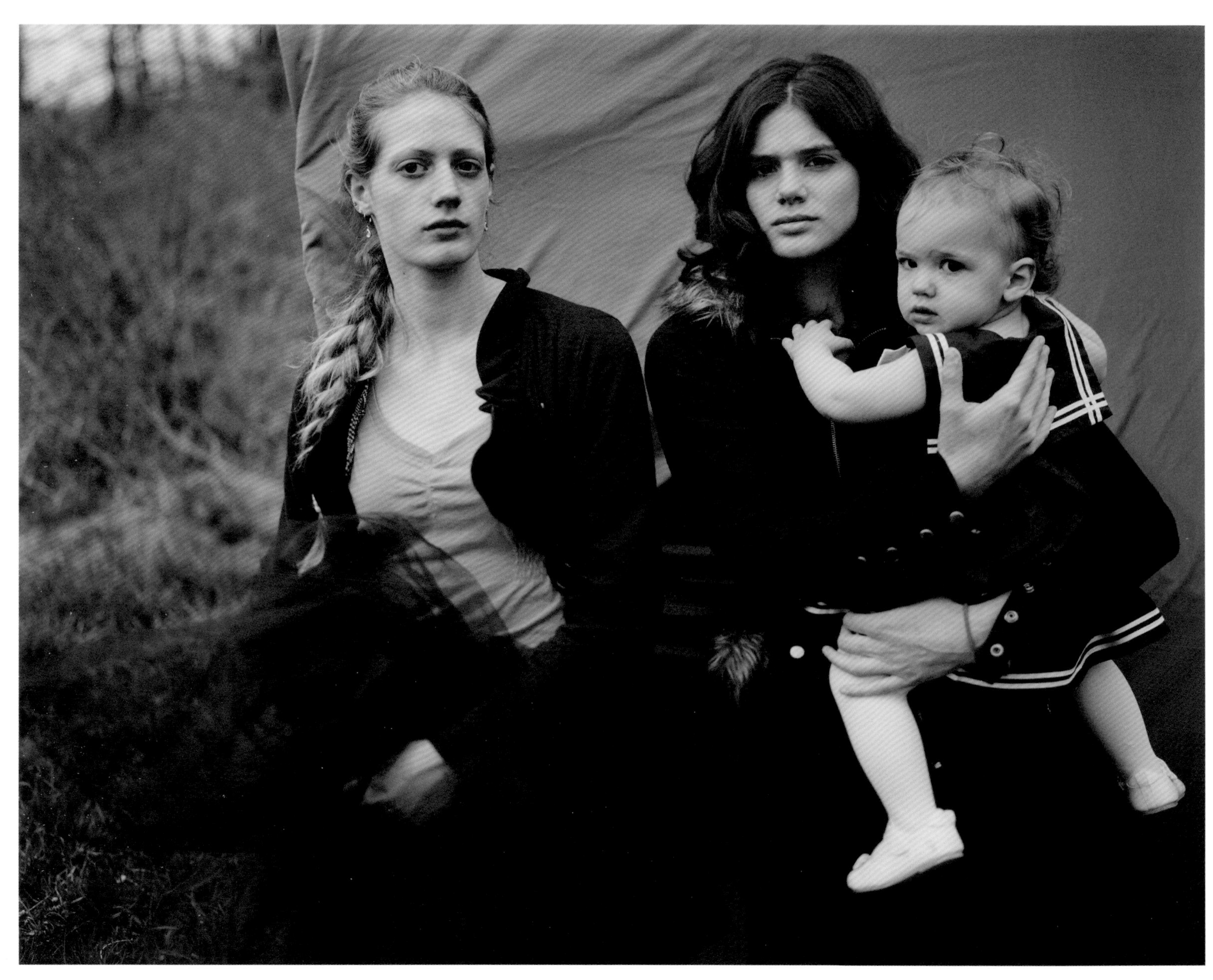

LYDIA PANAS
KITTY, CHRISTINE AND KIRA
APRIL 2011

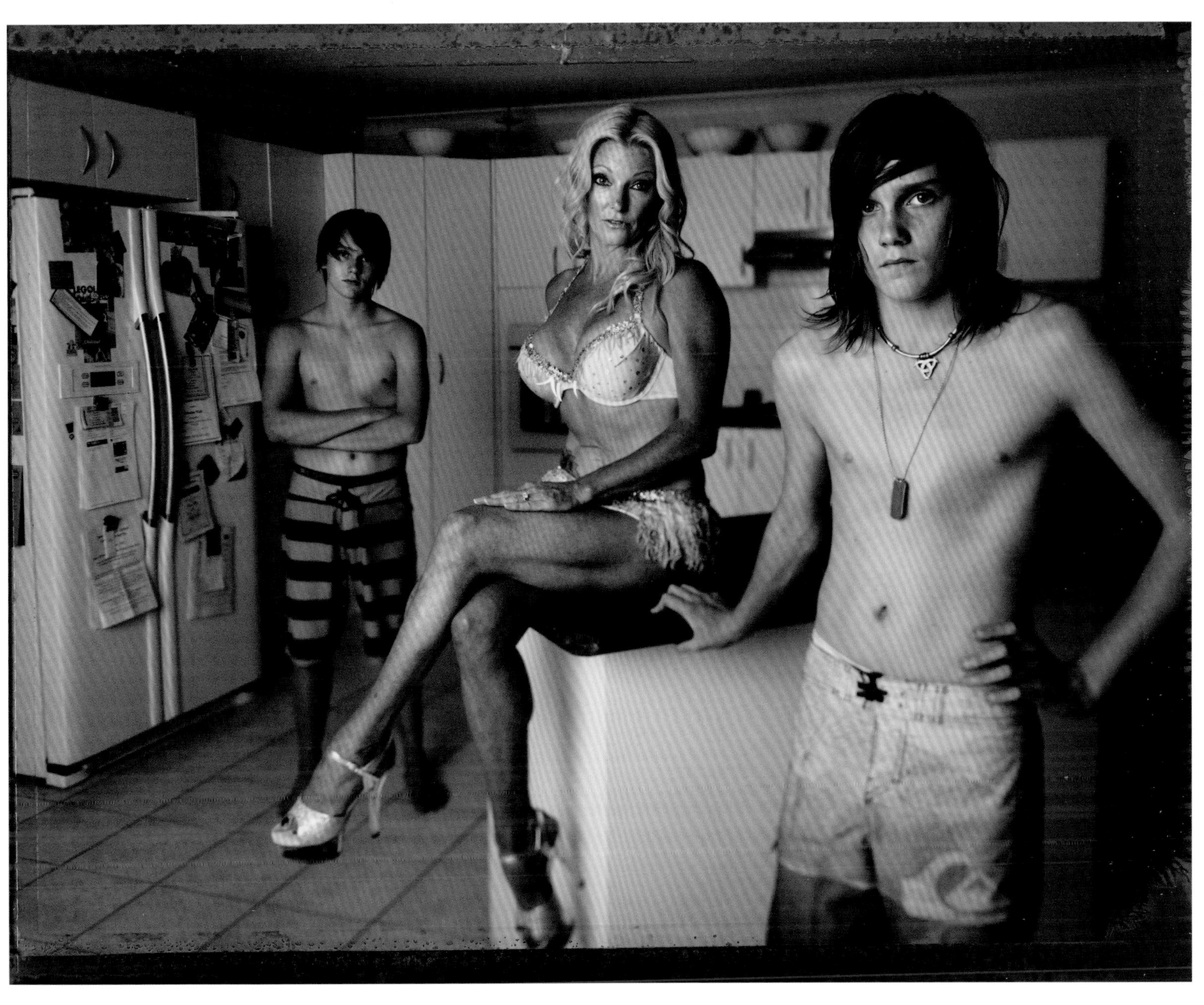

TOMASZ GUDZOWATY
KATY WITH SONS
FROM THE SERIES *NADA KUSTI – WORKING AGAINST THE DECLINE*
NOVEMBER 2011

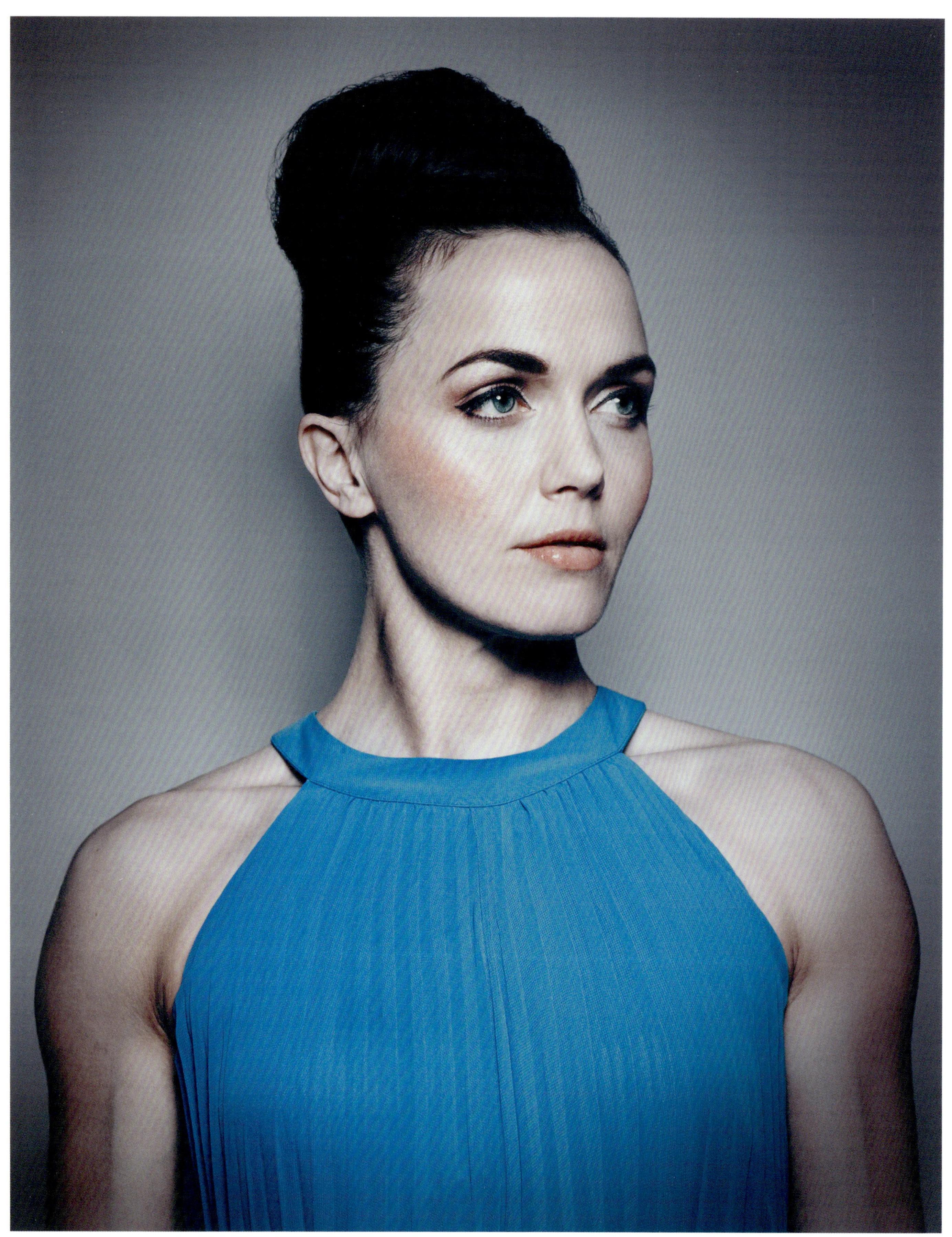

DAVID CLERIHEW
VICTORIA PENDLETON
APRIL 2012

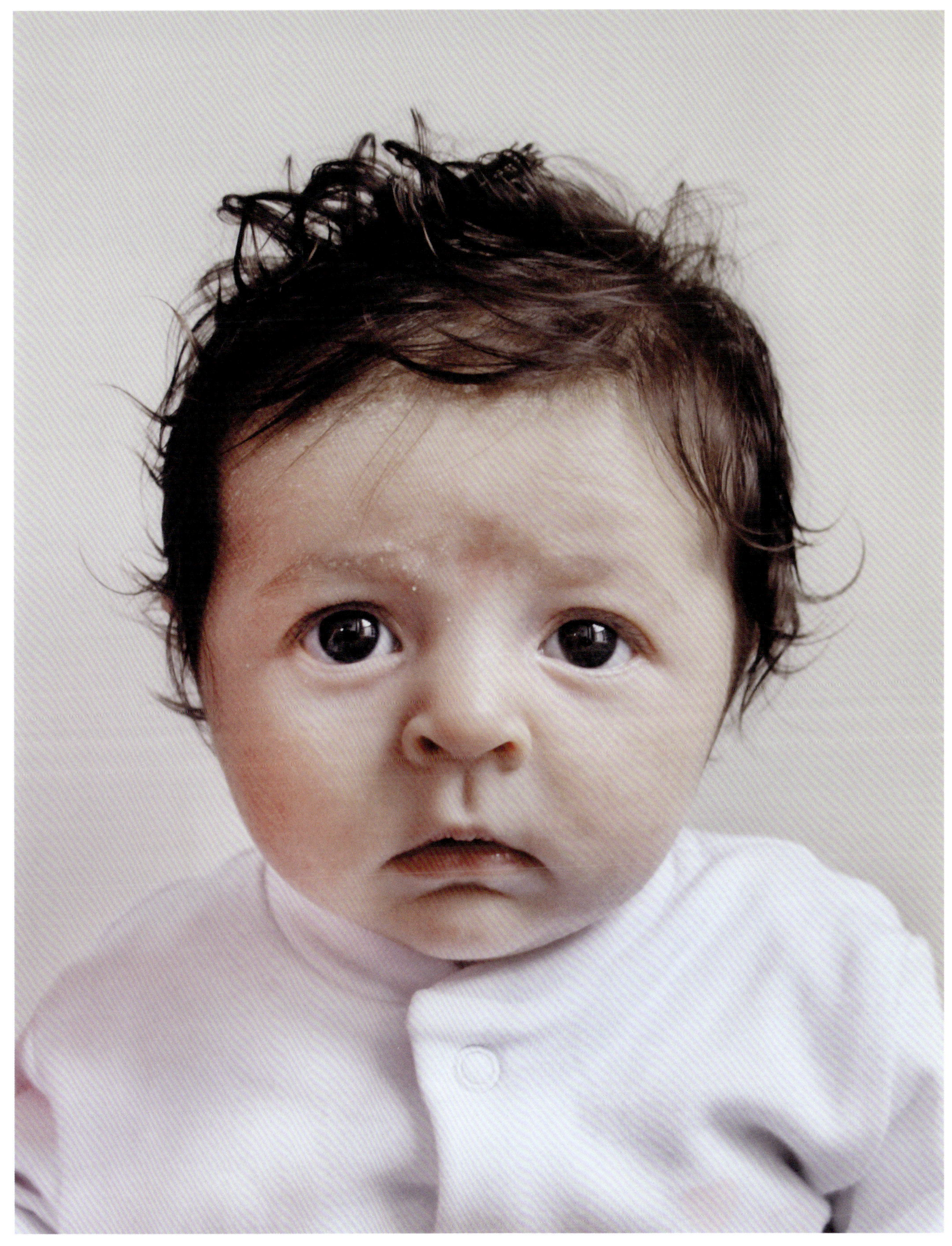

MARK MCEVOY
DAHLIA, 7 WEEKS
FROM THE SERIES *FAMILY PORTRAITS*
JUNE 2012

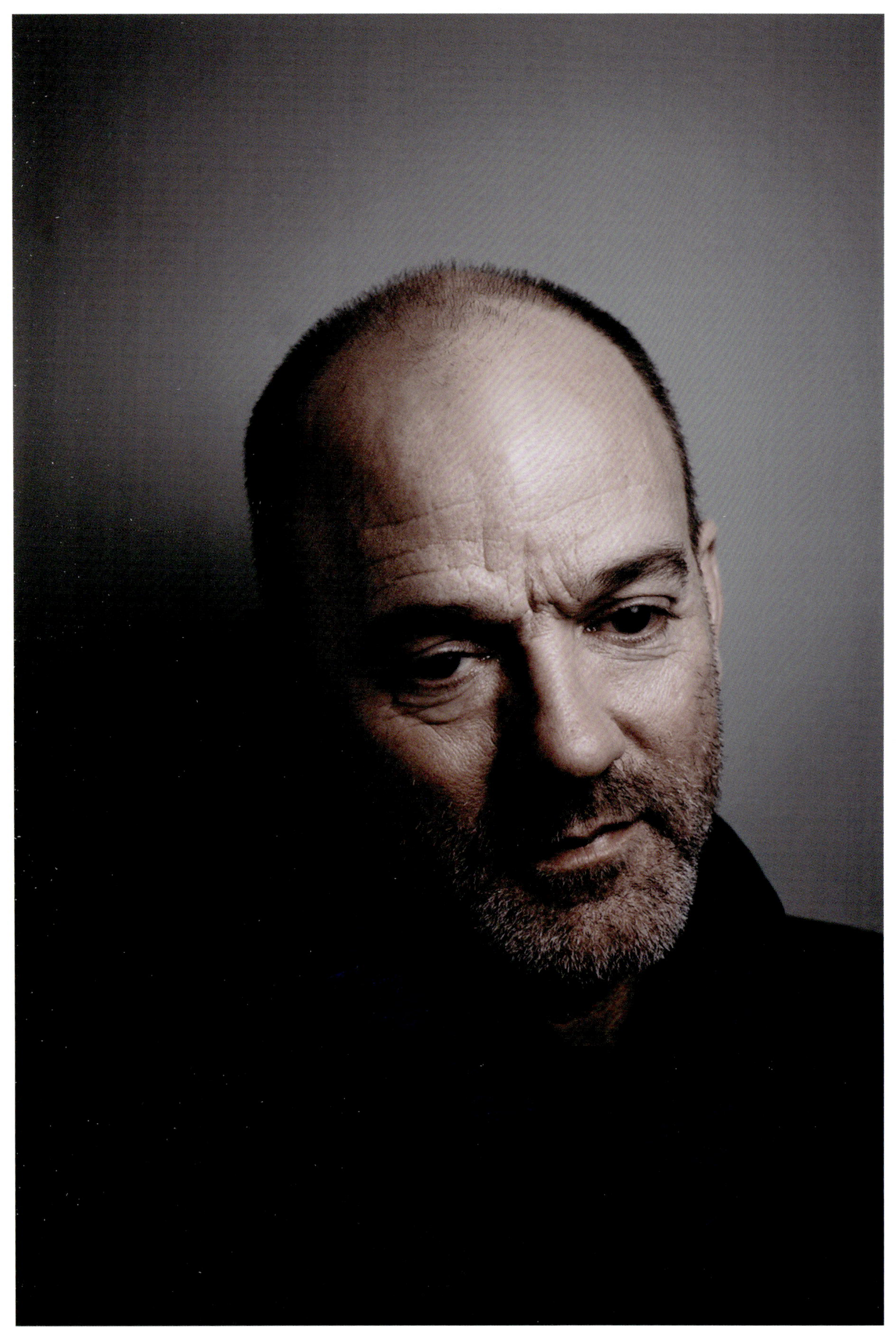

MATTHEW LLOYD
MICHAEL STIPE
FROM THE SERIES *FACES*
MARCH 2011

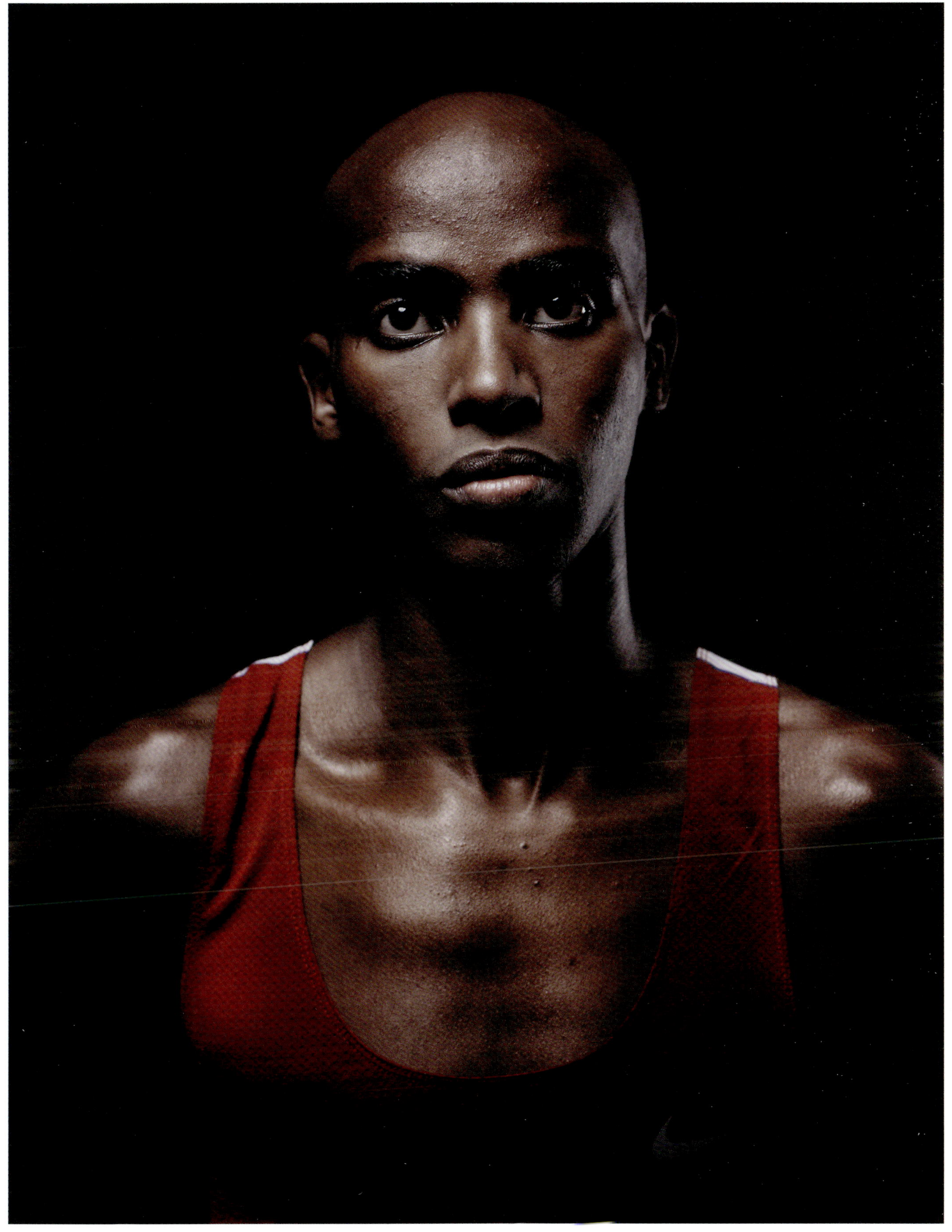

KATE PETERS
MO FARAH
FROM THE SERIES *OLYMPIANS*
MARCH 2012

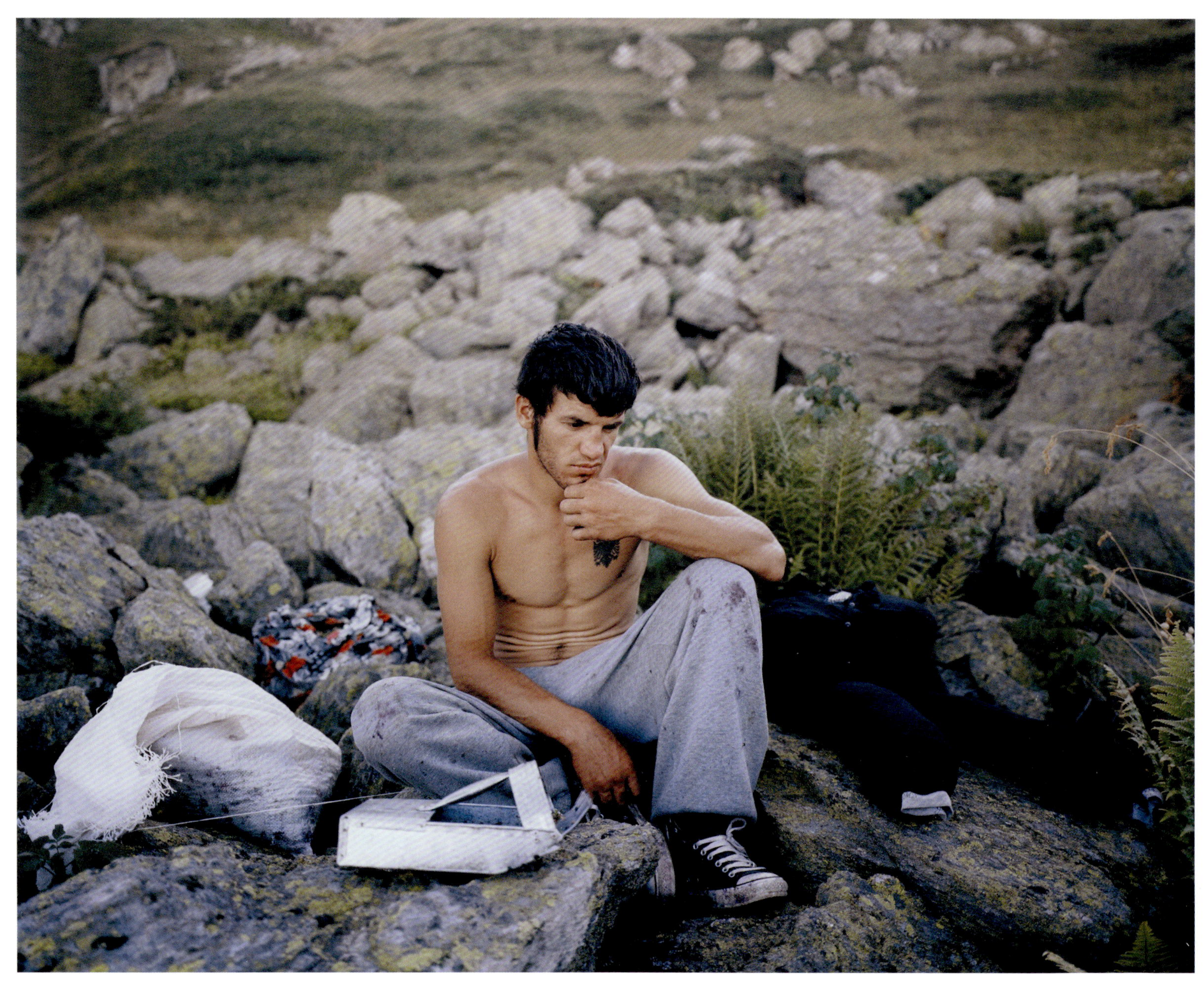

MARCO KESSELER
ARJANIT, IN HIDING FROM A BLOOD FEUD, KUKËS COUNTY
FROM THE SERIES *GJAKMARRJA: ALBANIA'S REVENGED BLOOD*
AUGUST 2011

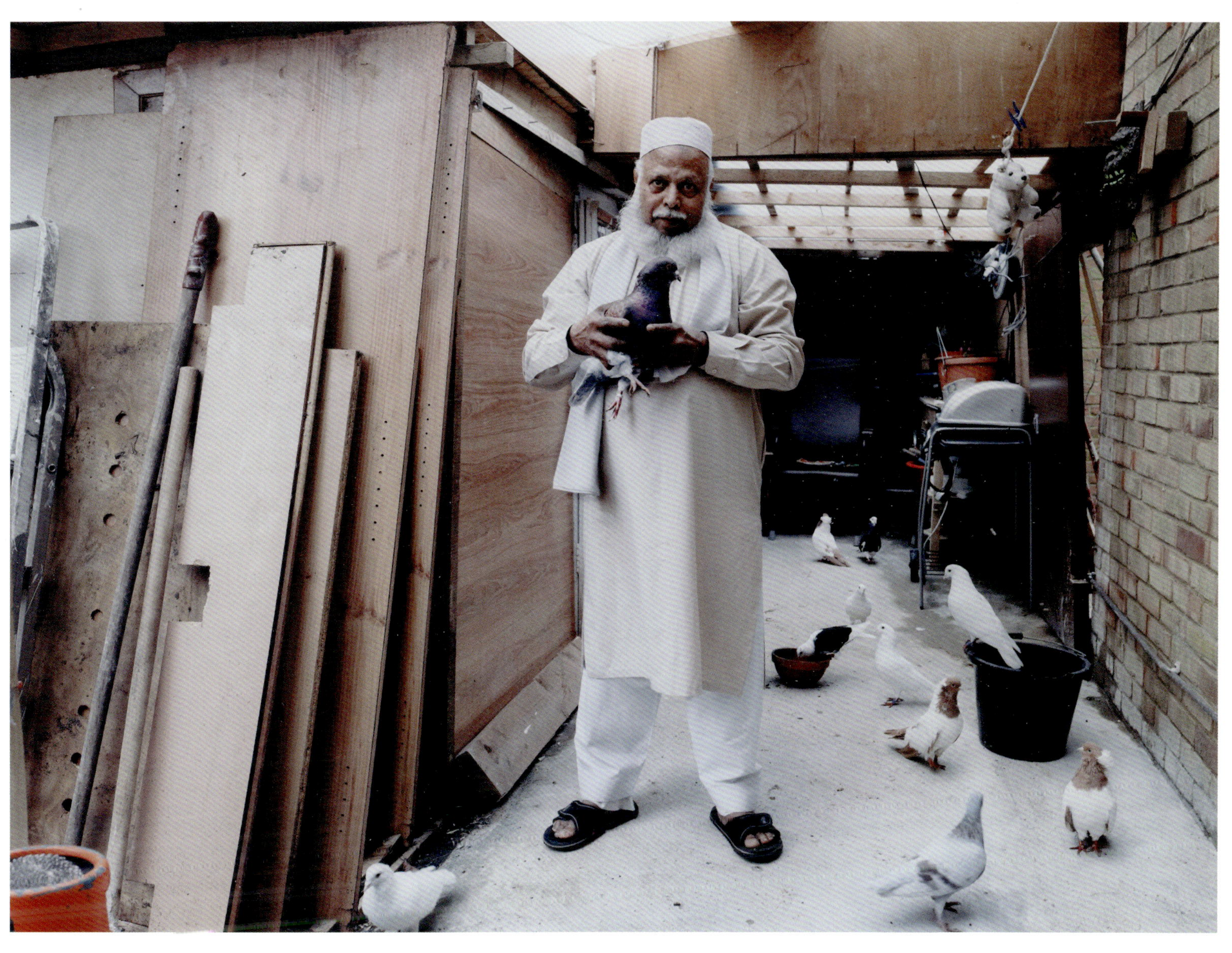

KEIRAN PERRY
MR EKLIAS
FROM THE SERIES *BRITAIN'S BACKYARD*
MARCH 2012

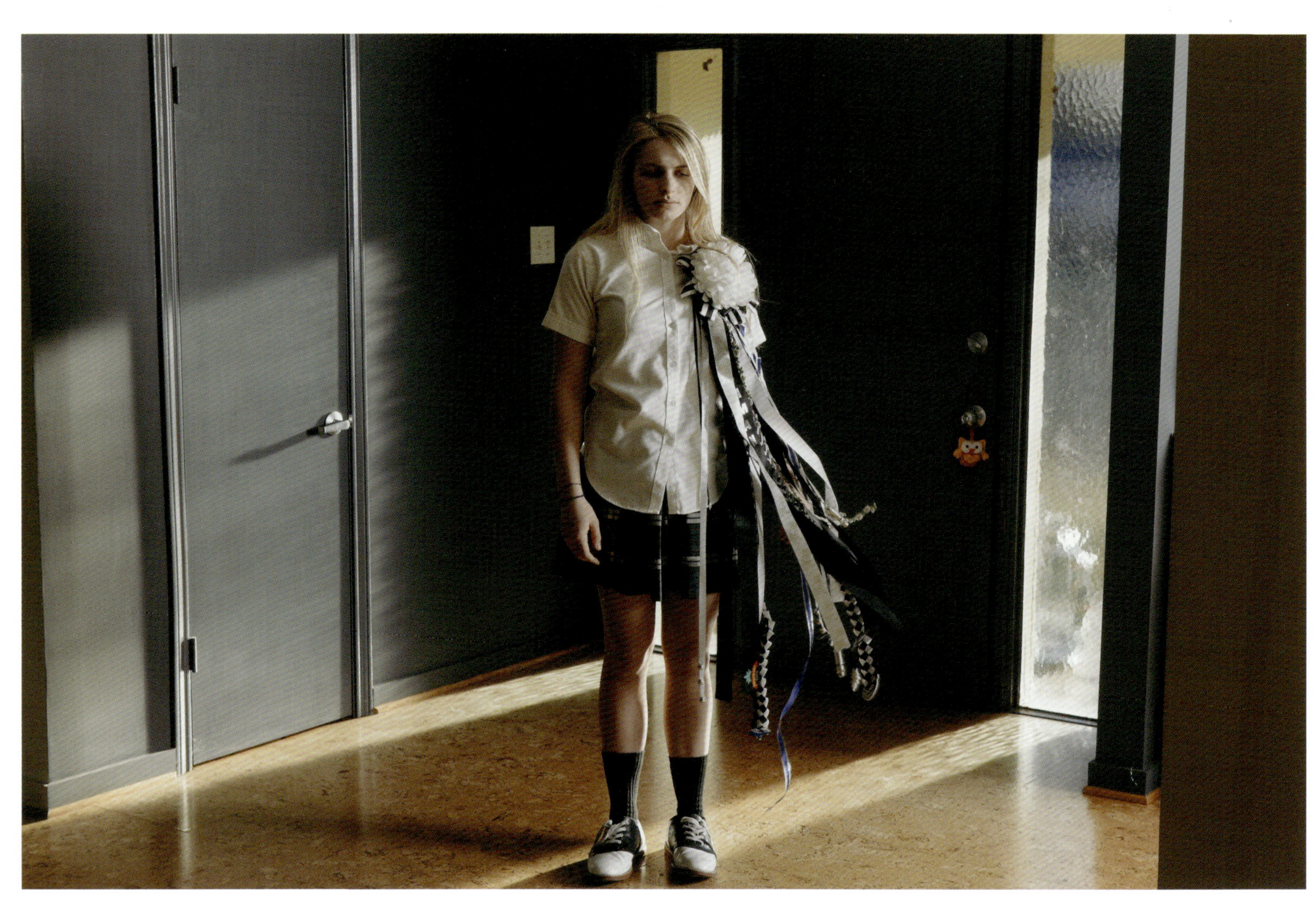

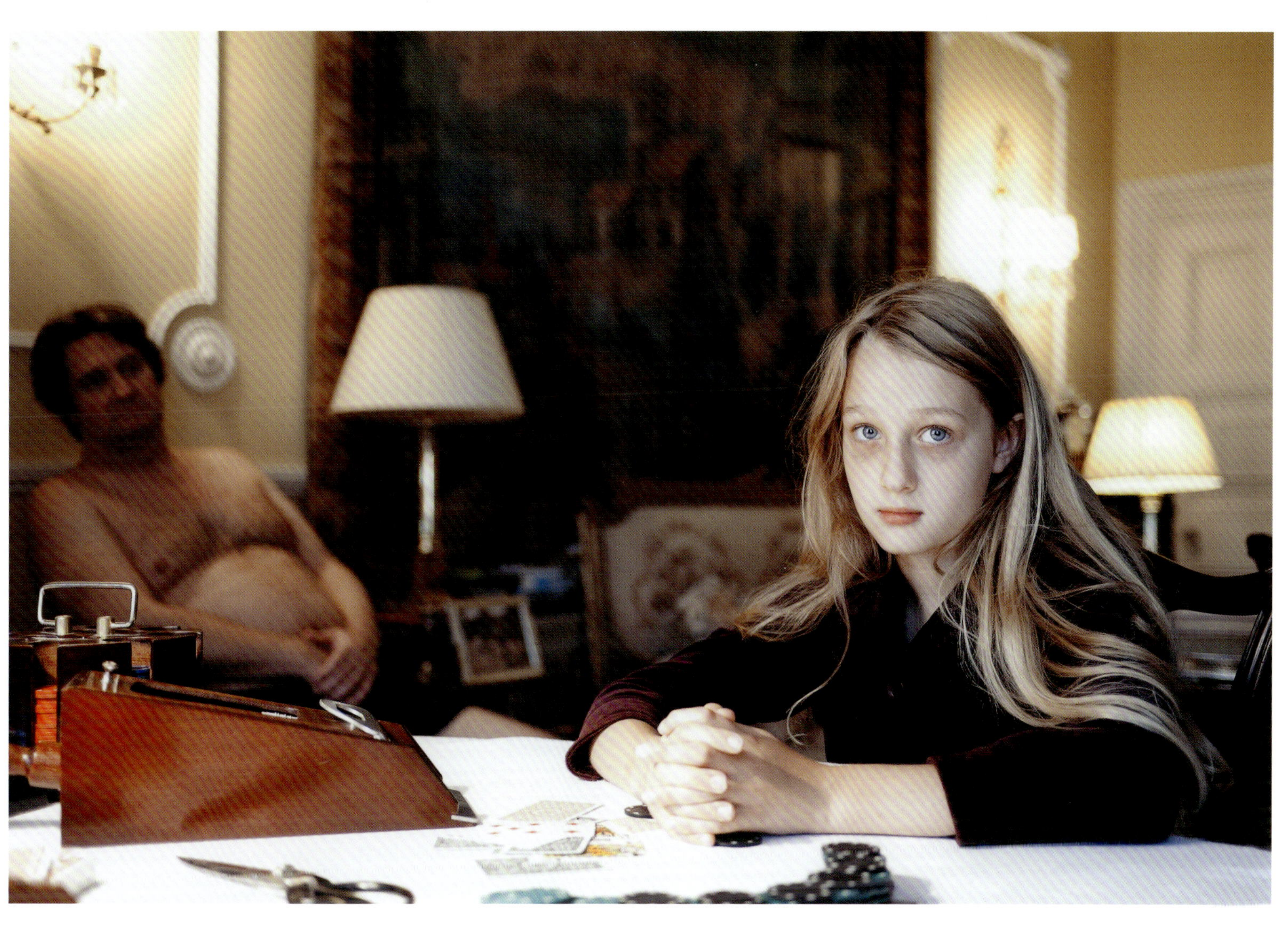

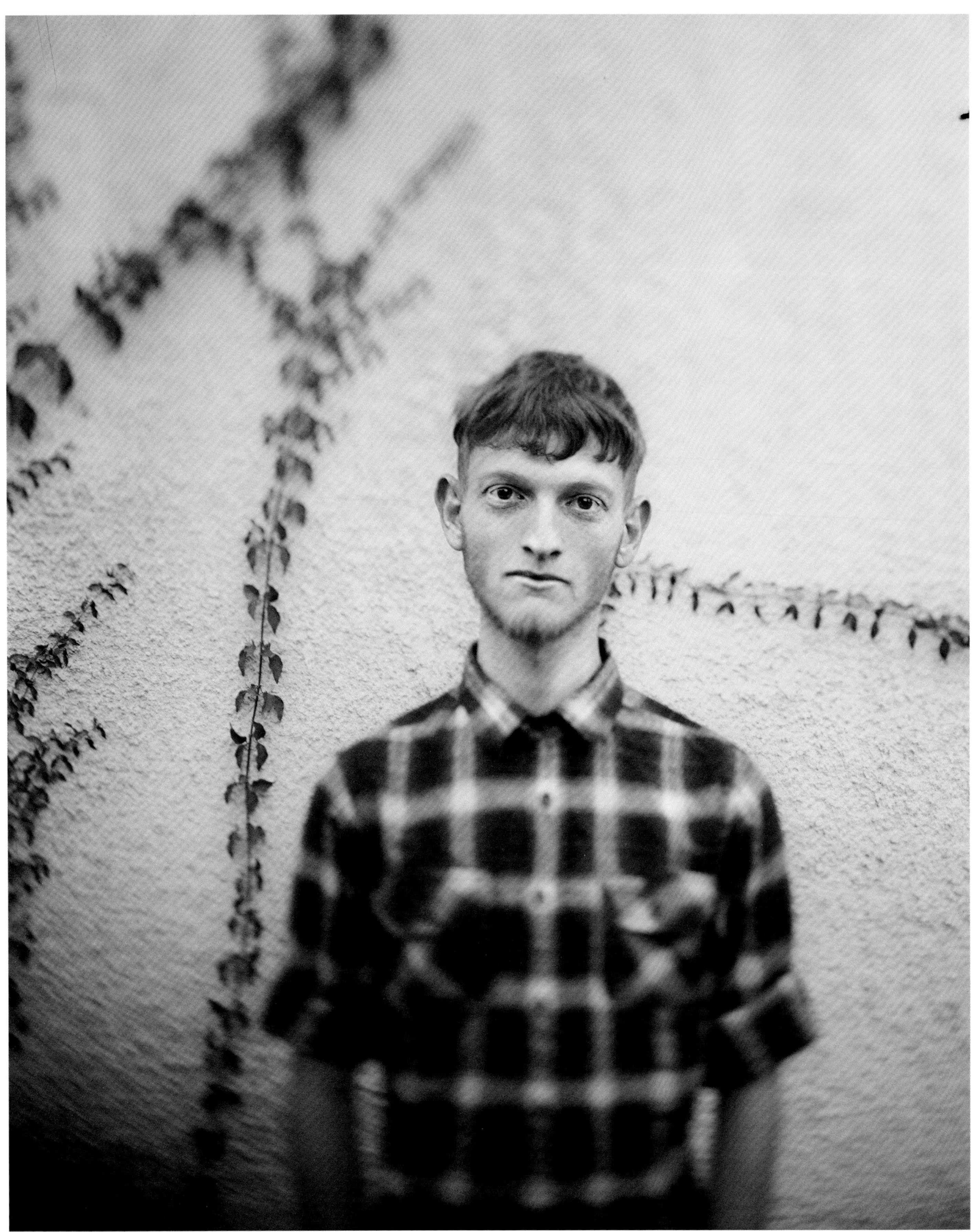

TAL BLUM
RAZ 2012
FROM THE SERIES *MEETINGS WITH REMARKABLE MAN*
JANUARY 2012

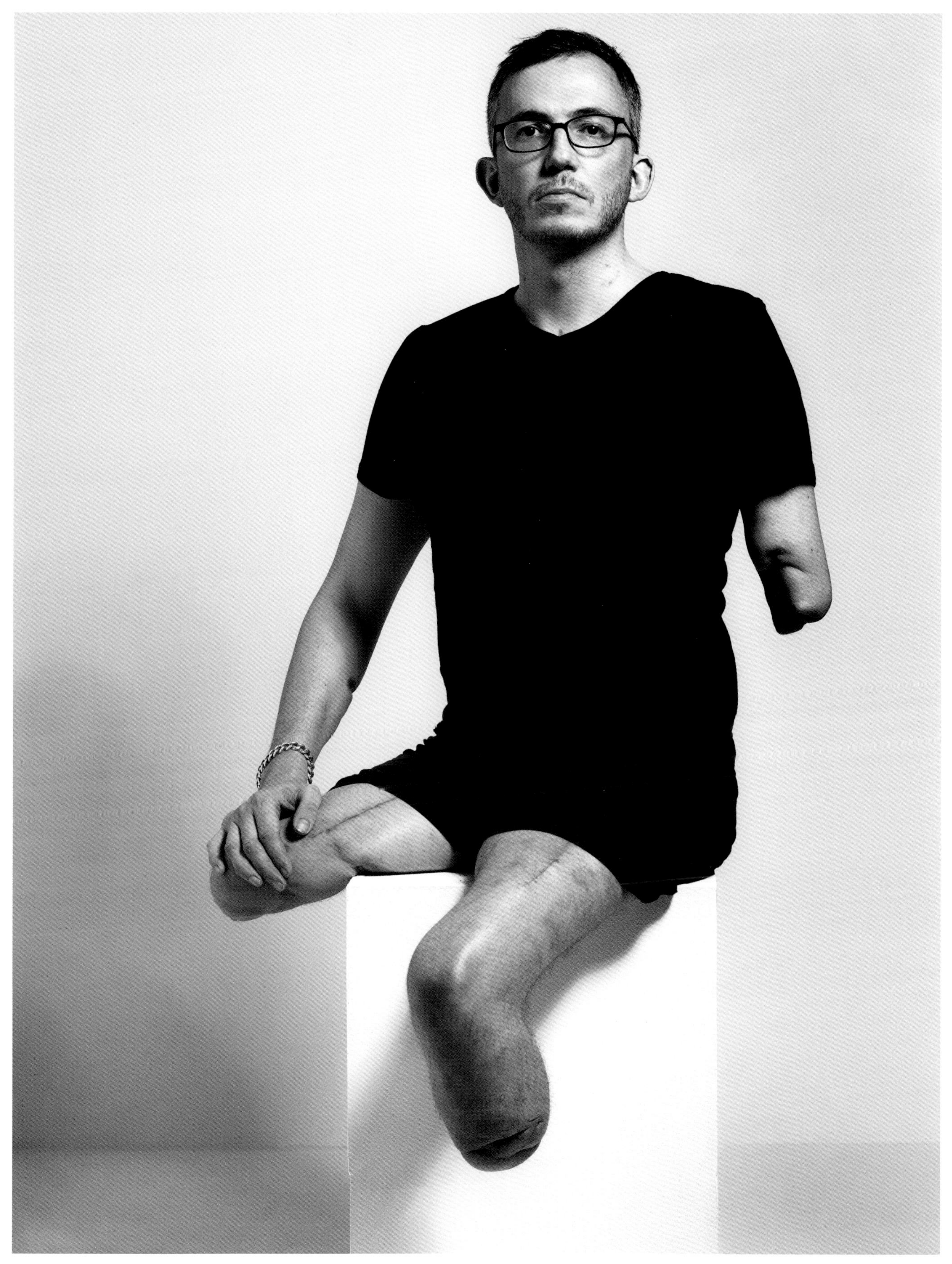

GILES DULEY
BECOMING THE STORY, SELF-PORTRAIT
OCTOBER 2011

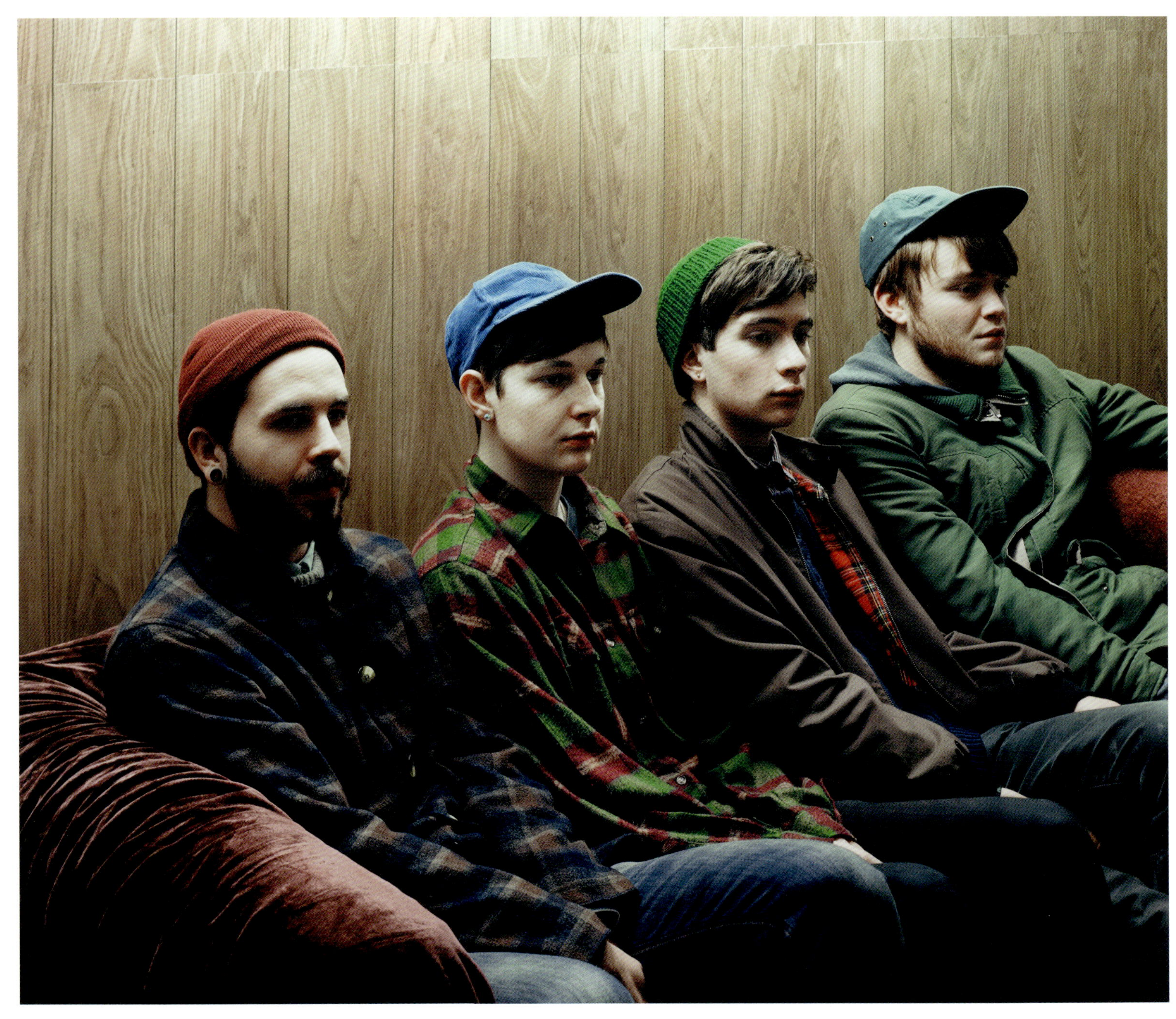

DAVID STEWART
FOUR HATS
FROM THE SERIES *TEENAGE PRE-OCCUPATION*
JANUARY 2012

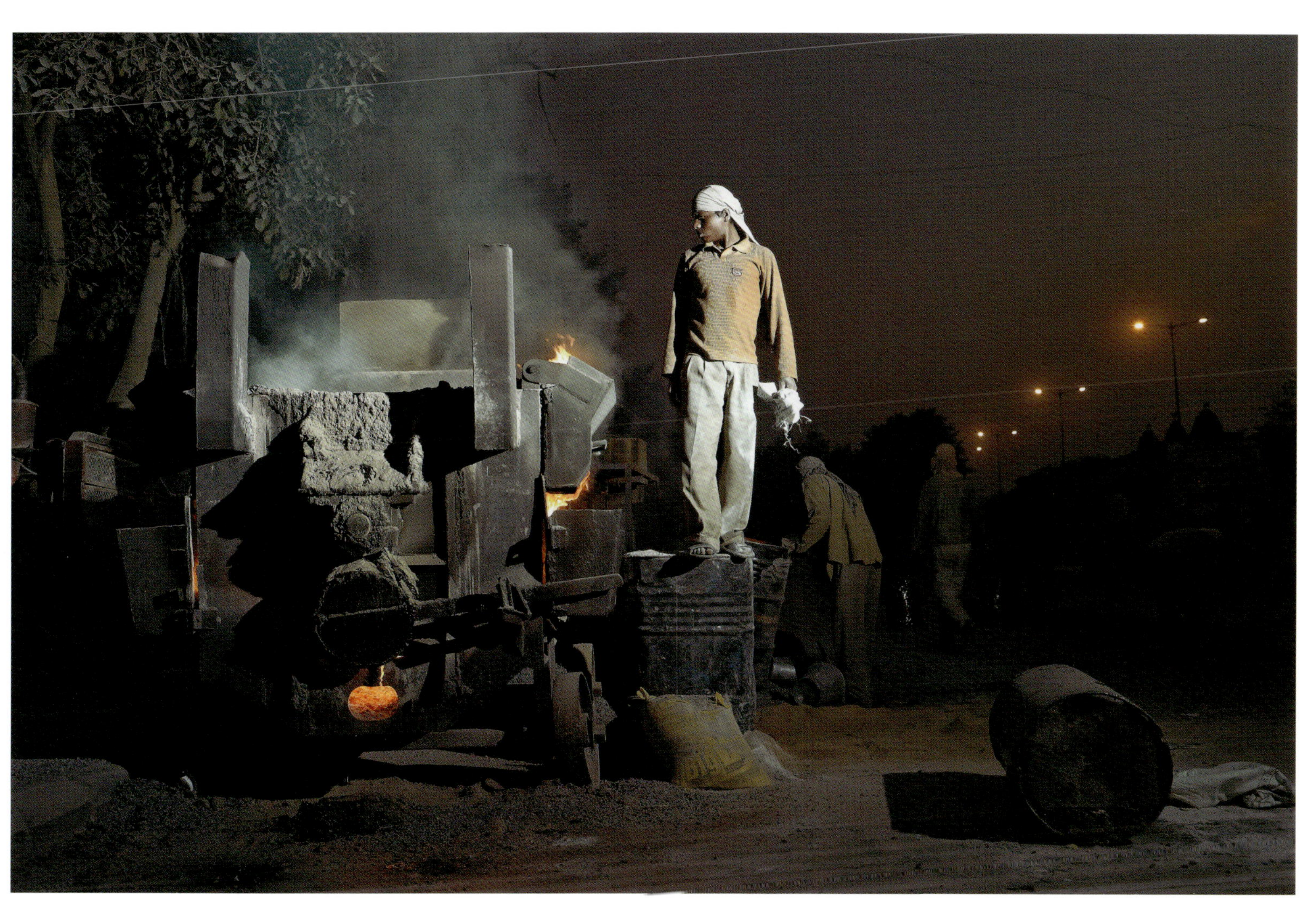

JEREMY RATA
ROAD WORKERS IN OLD DELHI
FEBRUARY 2011

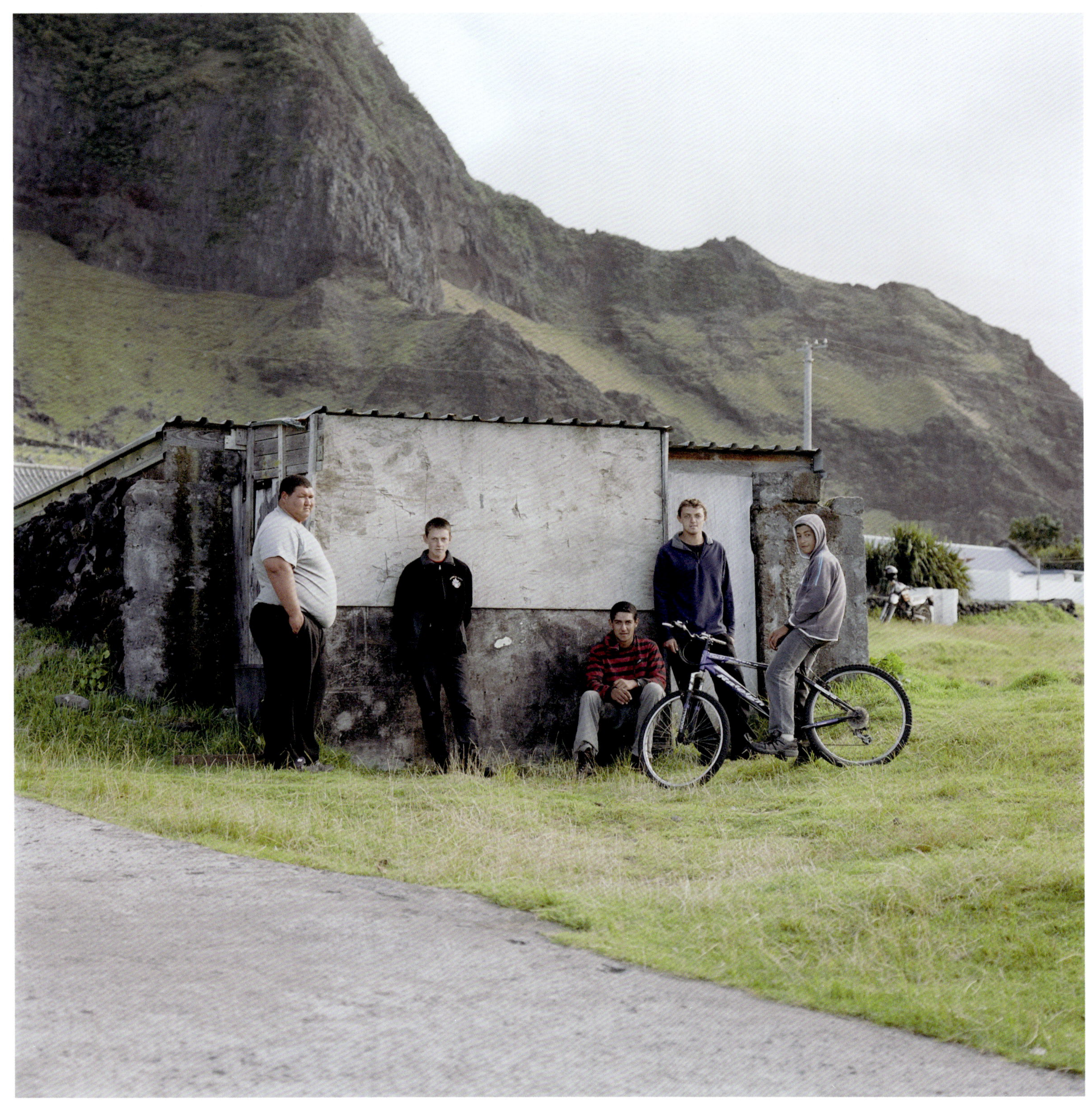

JON TONKS

THE BOYS OF TRISTAN DA CUNHA

FROM THE SERIES *TRISTAN DA CUNHA, PART OF THE EMPIRE PROJECT*

FEBRUARY 2011

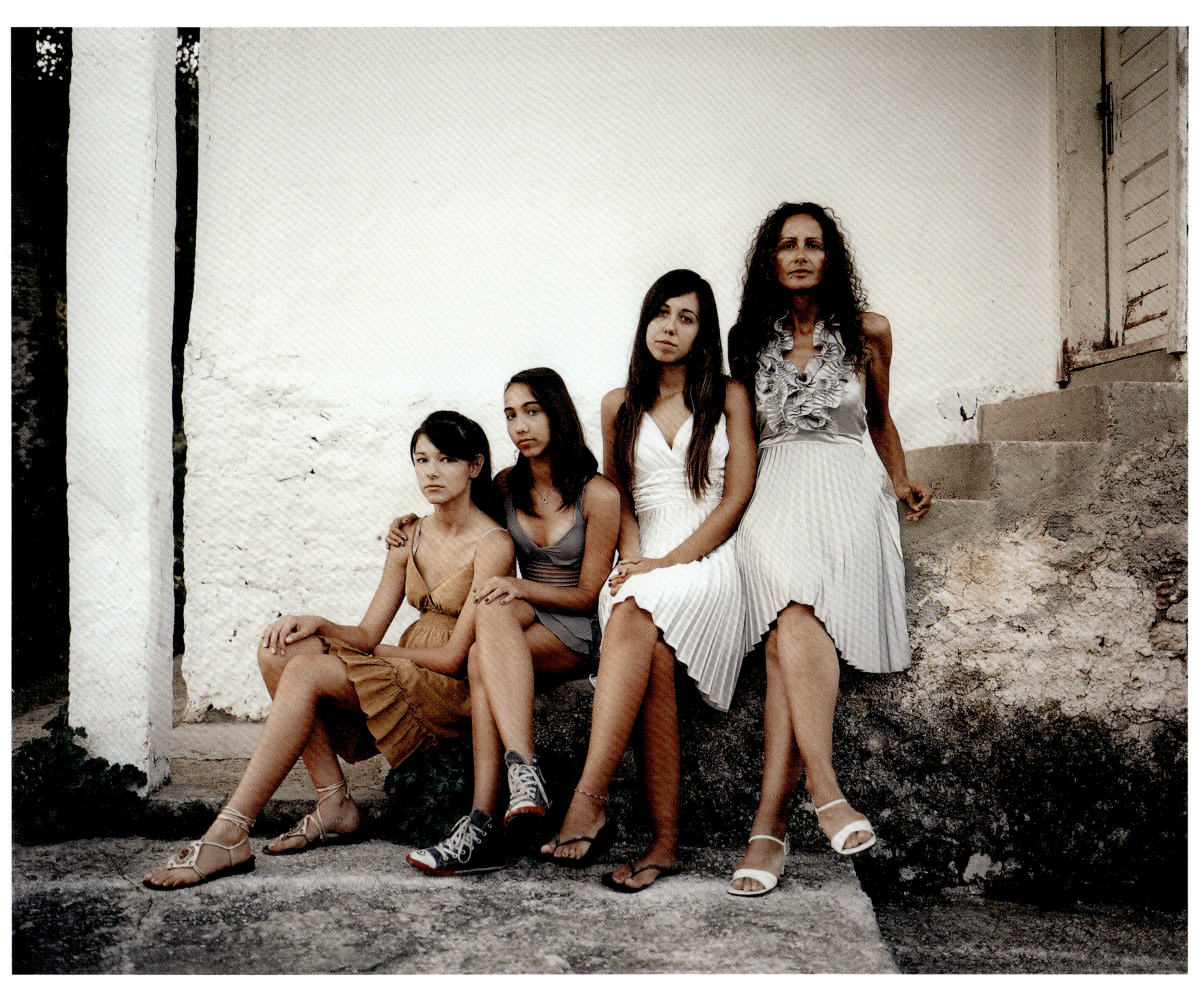

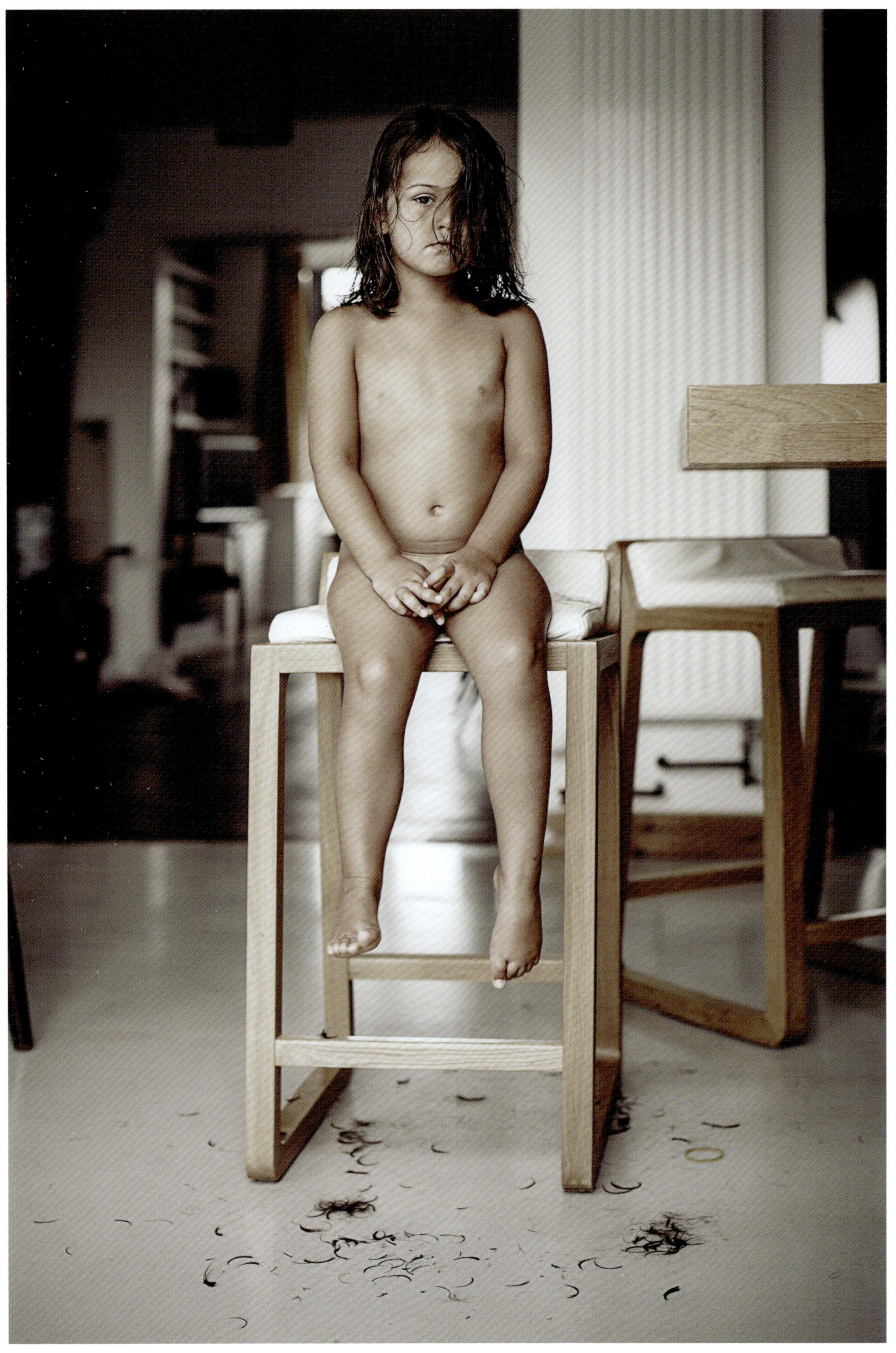

42

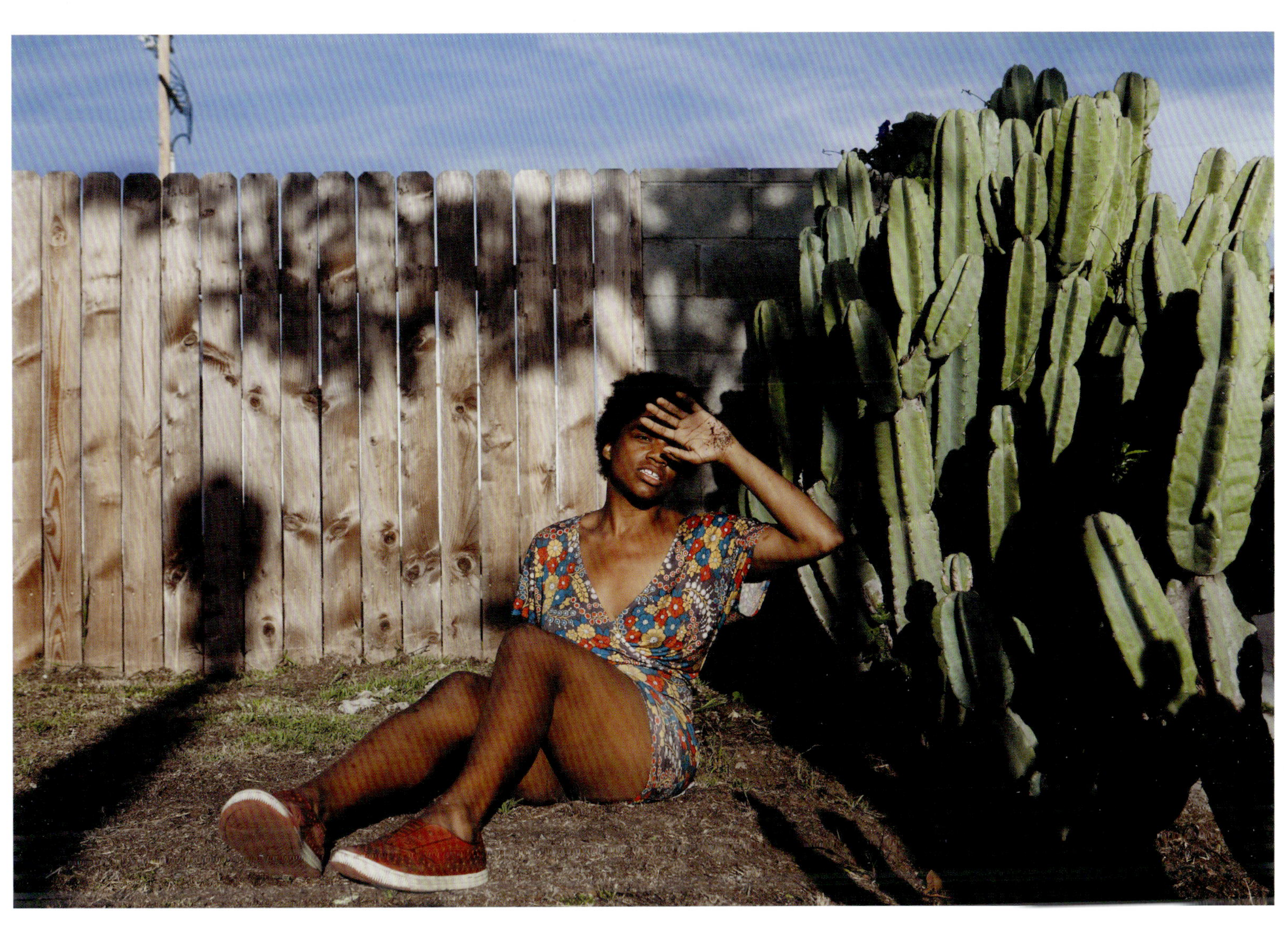

43

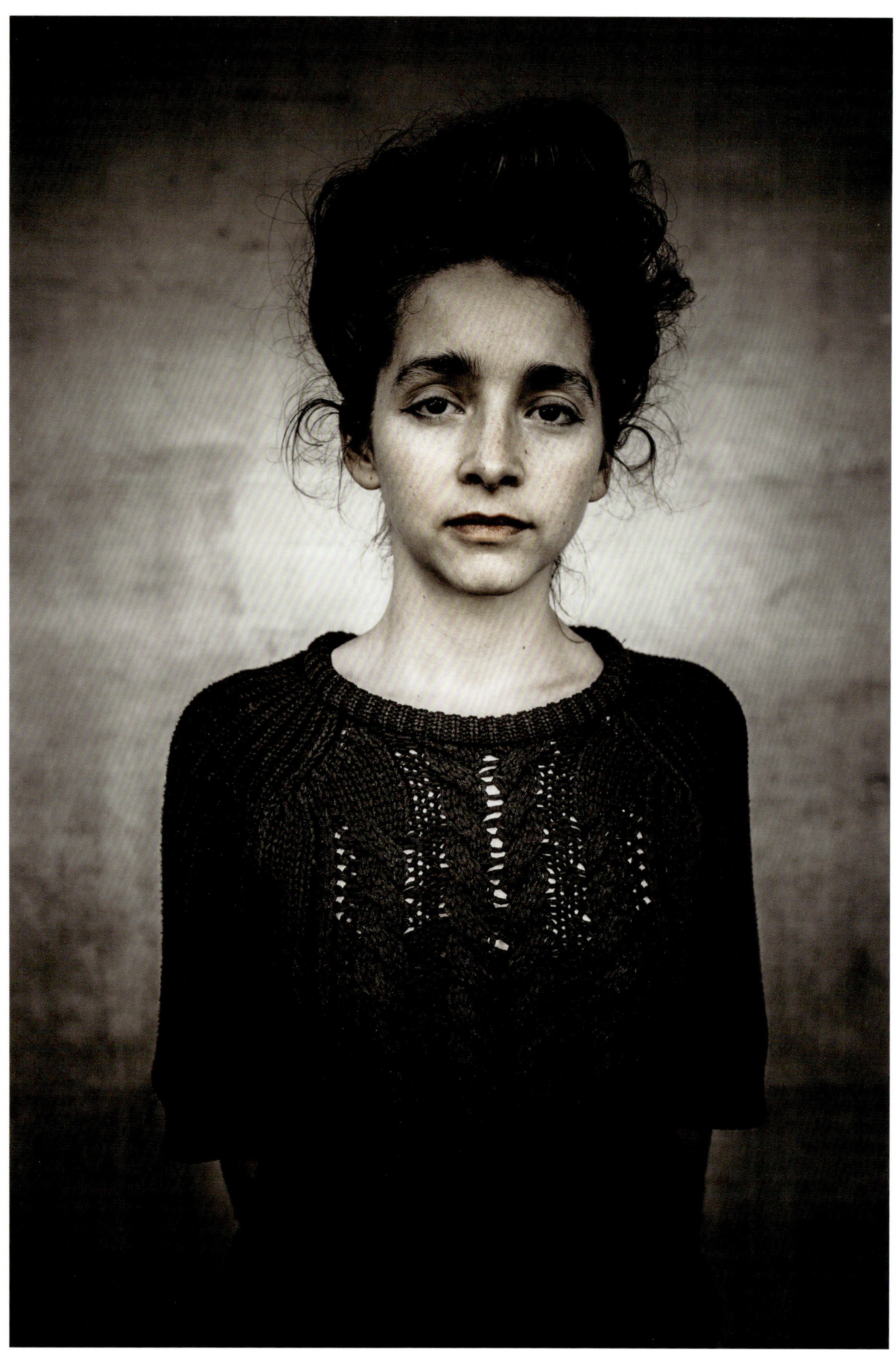

PEER LINDGREEN
JULIE HILL
MAY 2012

44

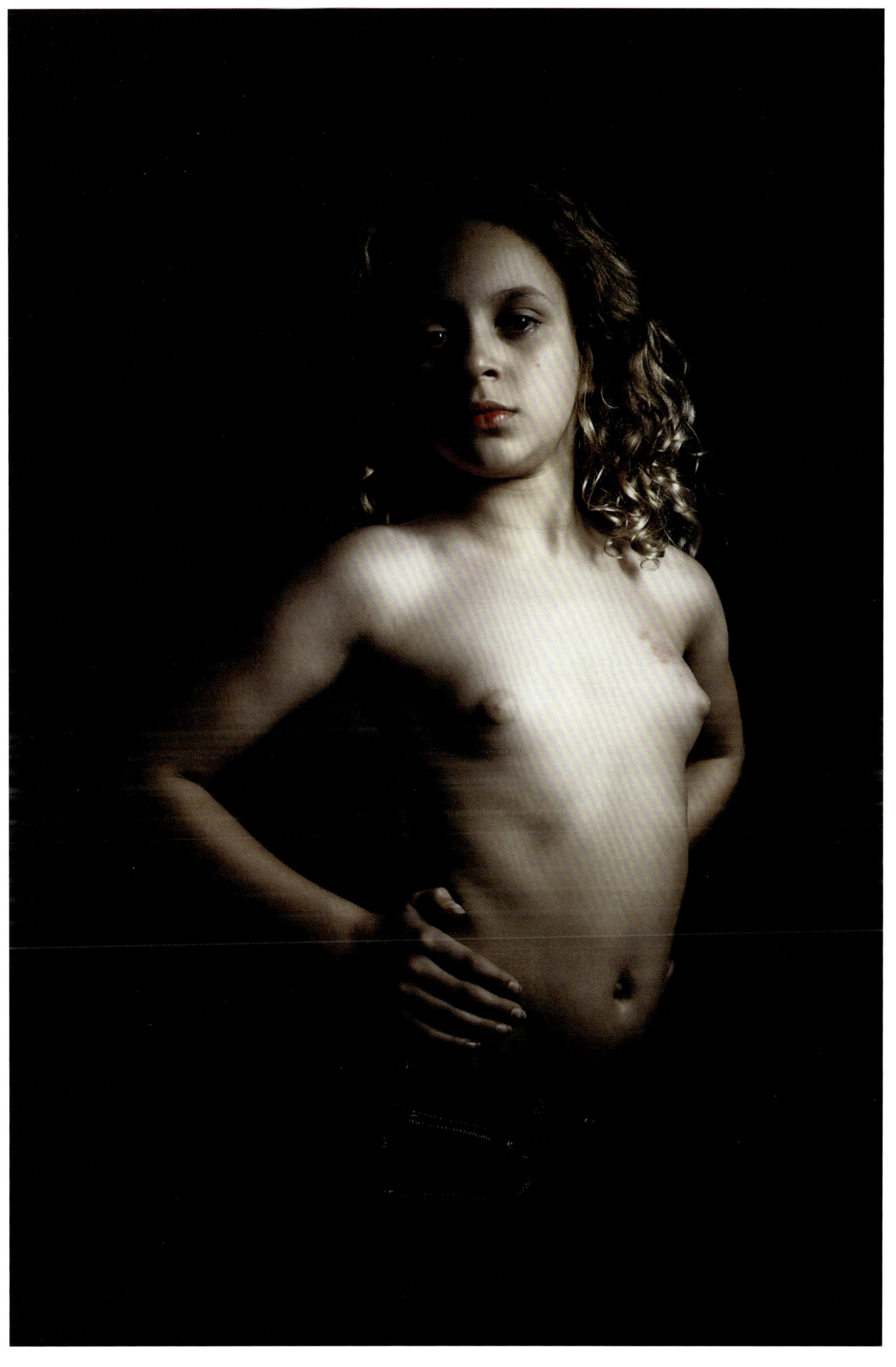

INEKE SCHOONHEYT
SENNA
FROM THE SERIES *THE BEAUTY AND THE SPIRIT*
NOVEMBER 2011

45

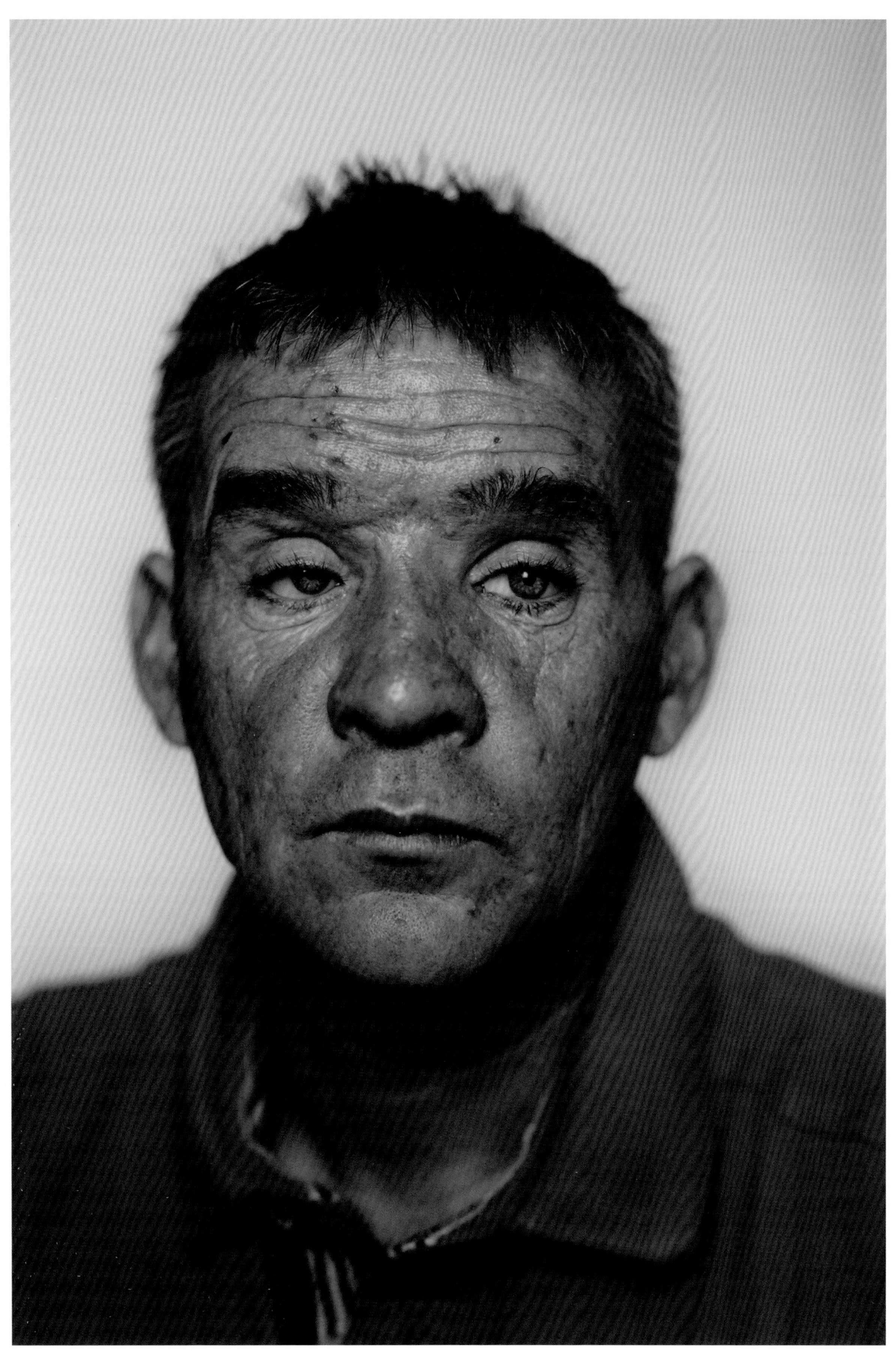

JUSTIN SUTCLIFFE
PC DAVID RATHBAND
FROM THE SERIES *BURNT BY LIMELIGHT*
JULY 2011

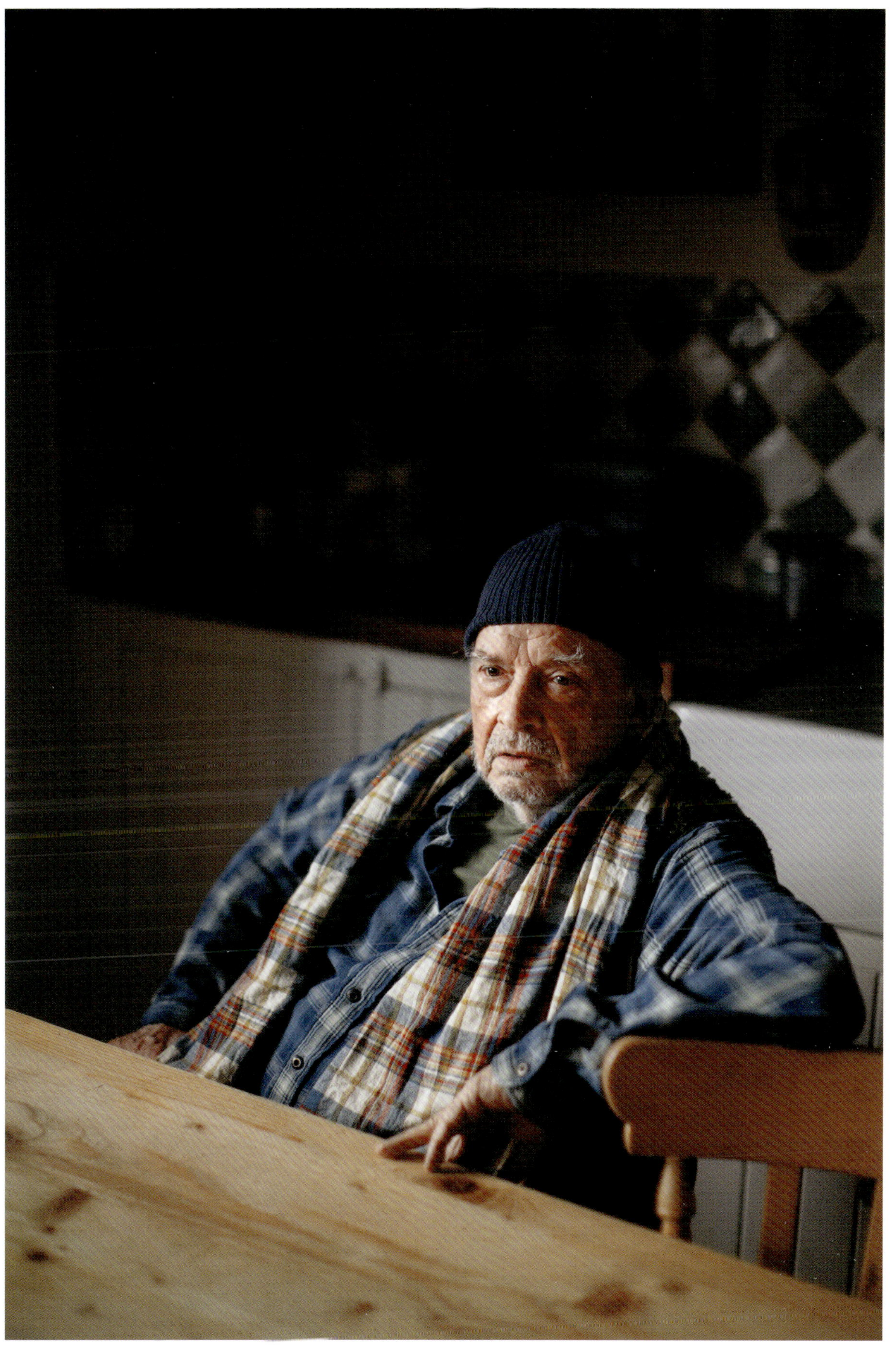

RICK MORRIS PUSHINSKY
DAVID BAILEY
DECEMBER 2011

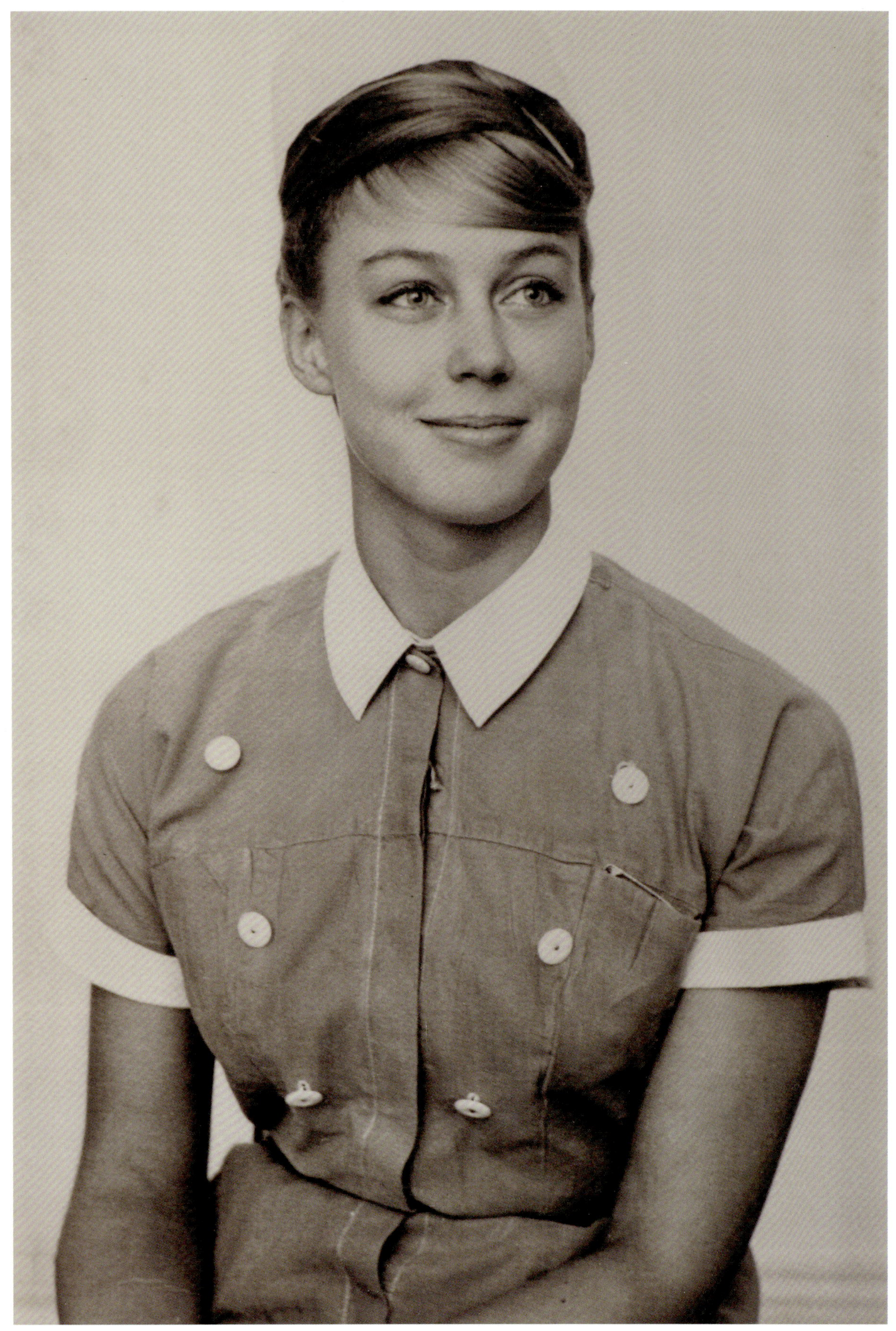

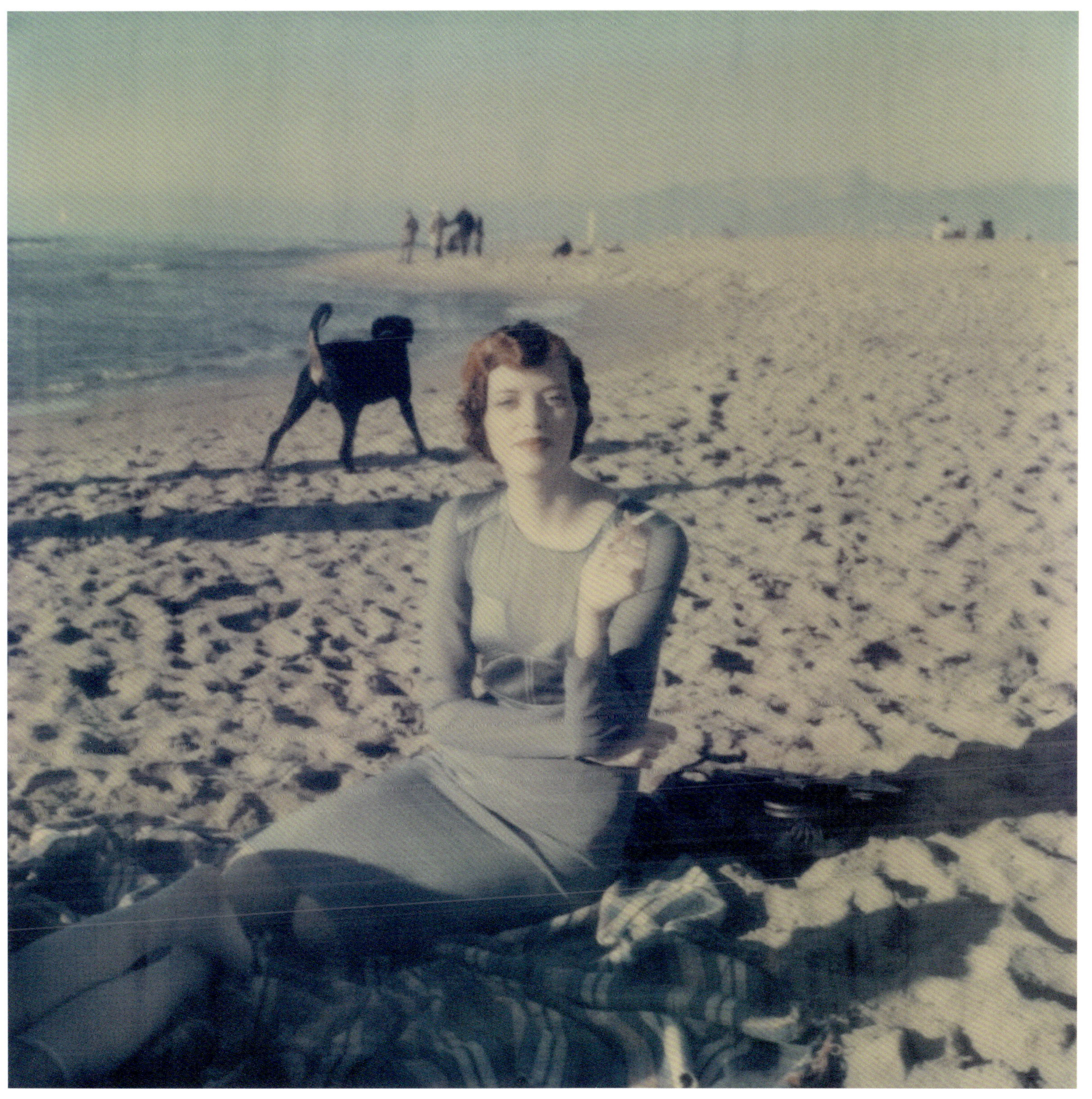

ALICE PAVESI FIORI
LOLA SMOKING
FROM THE SERIES OFF THE SET
FEBRUARY 2011

MARTINE HOUGHTON
A NEW ACQUISITION (PAUL FRECKER)
MARCH 2012

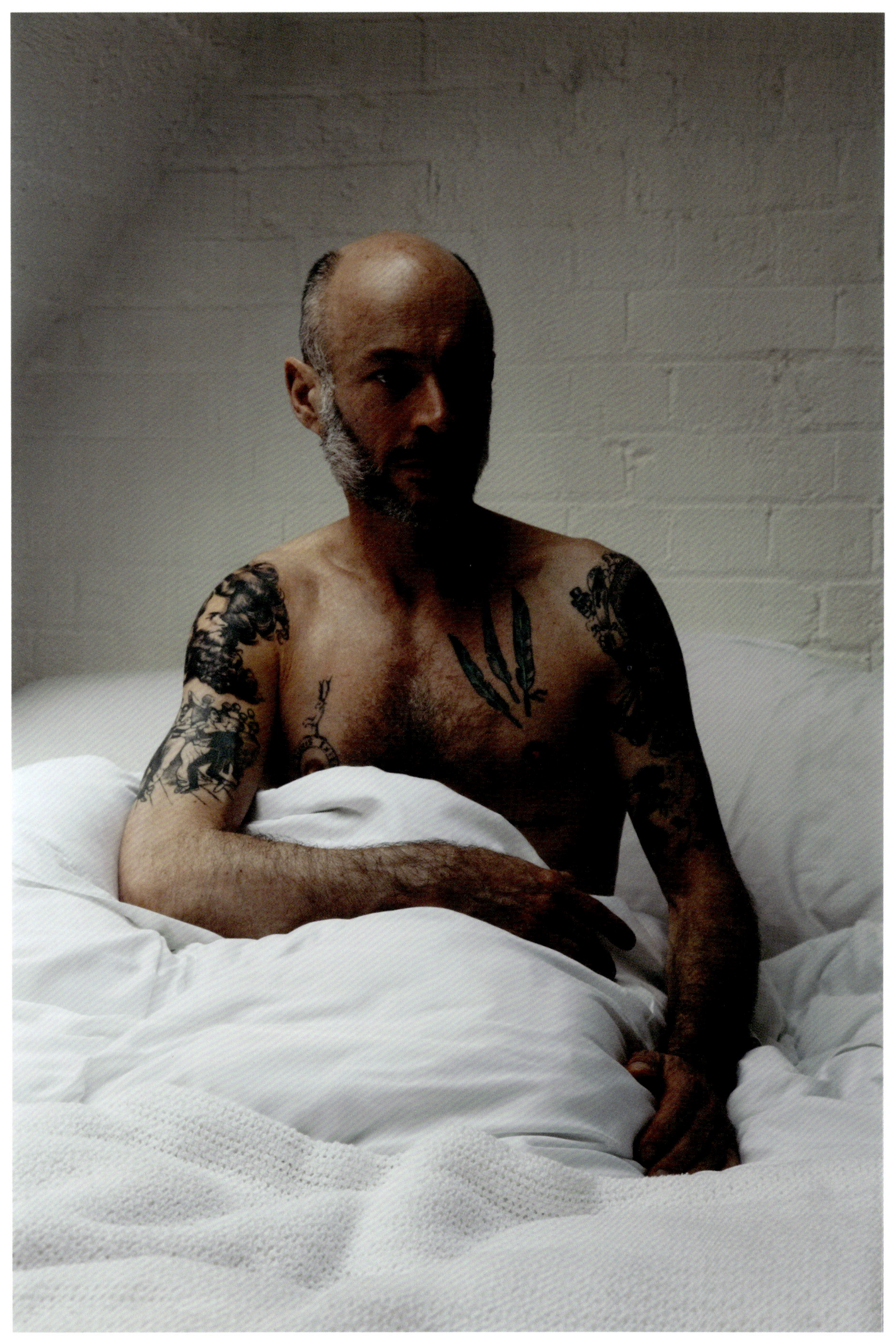

50

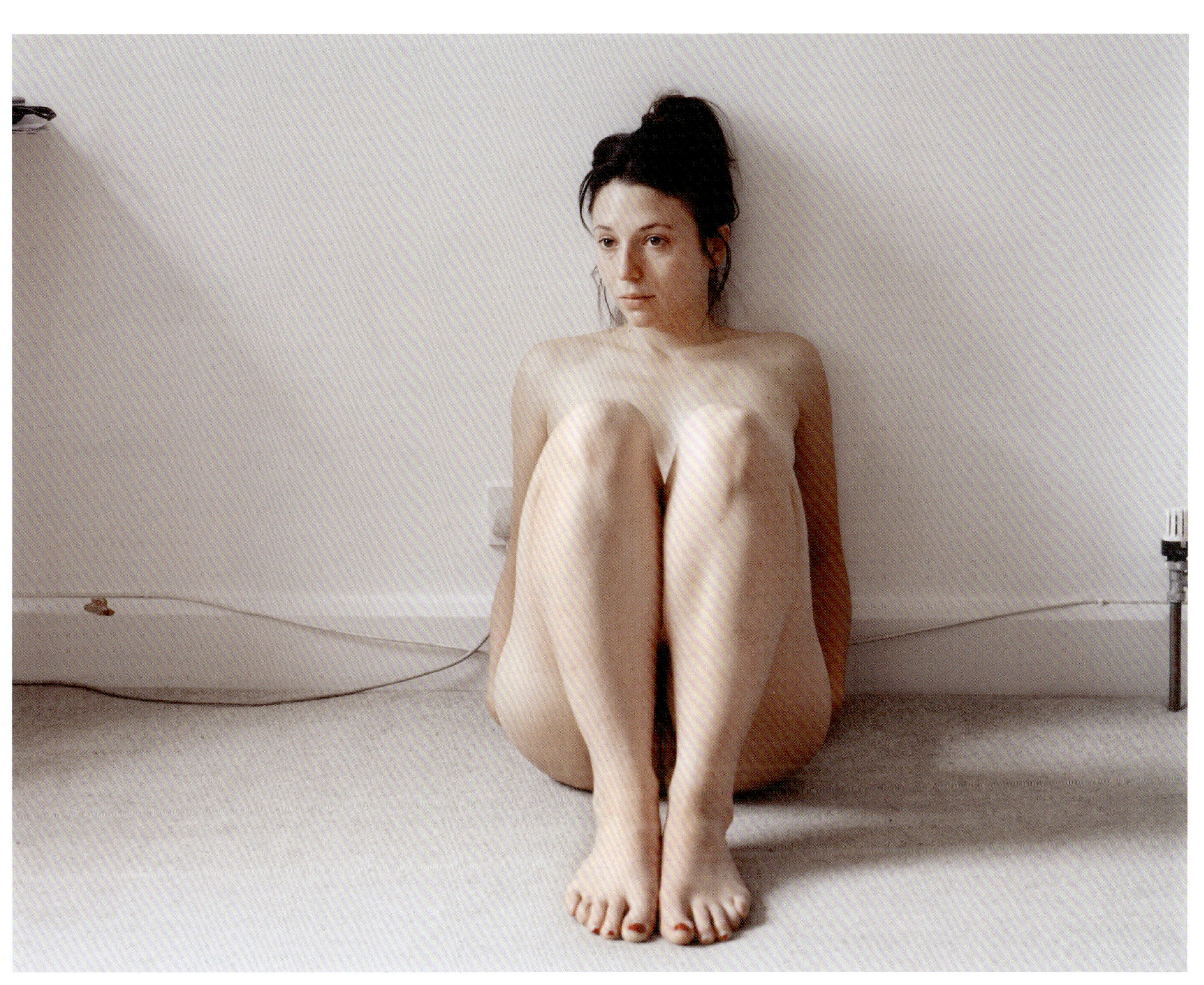

PHOEBE THEODORA
ONE SUMMER IN LONDON
JUNE 2012

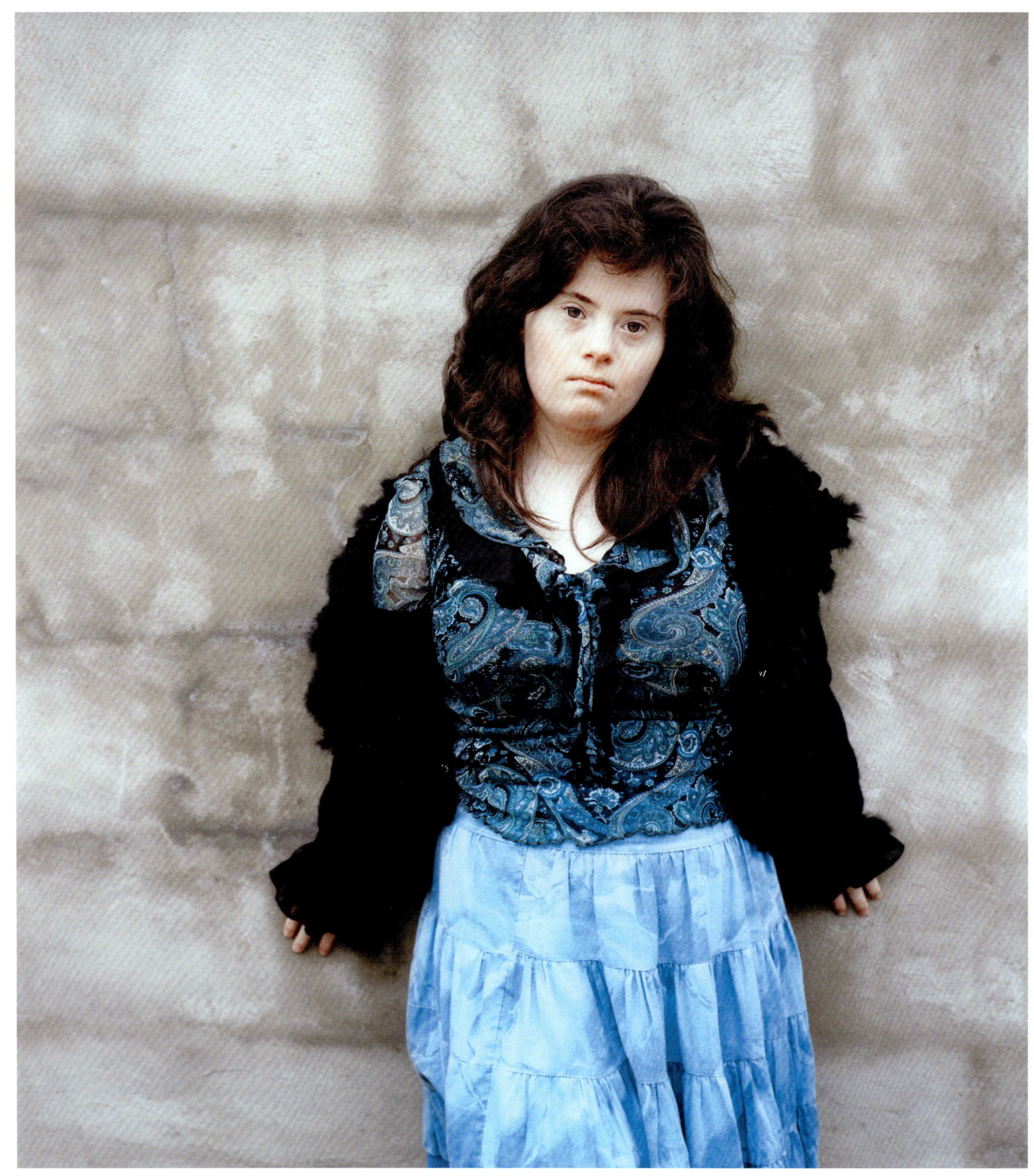

FIONA YARON-FIELD
BECOMING ANNALIE
FROM THE SERIES *BECOMING*
OCTOBER 2011

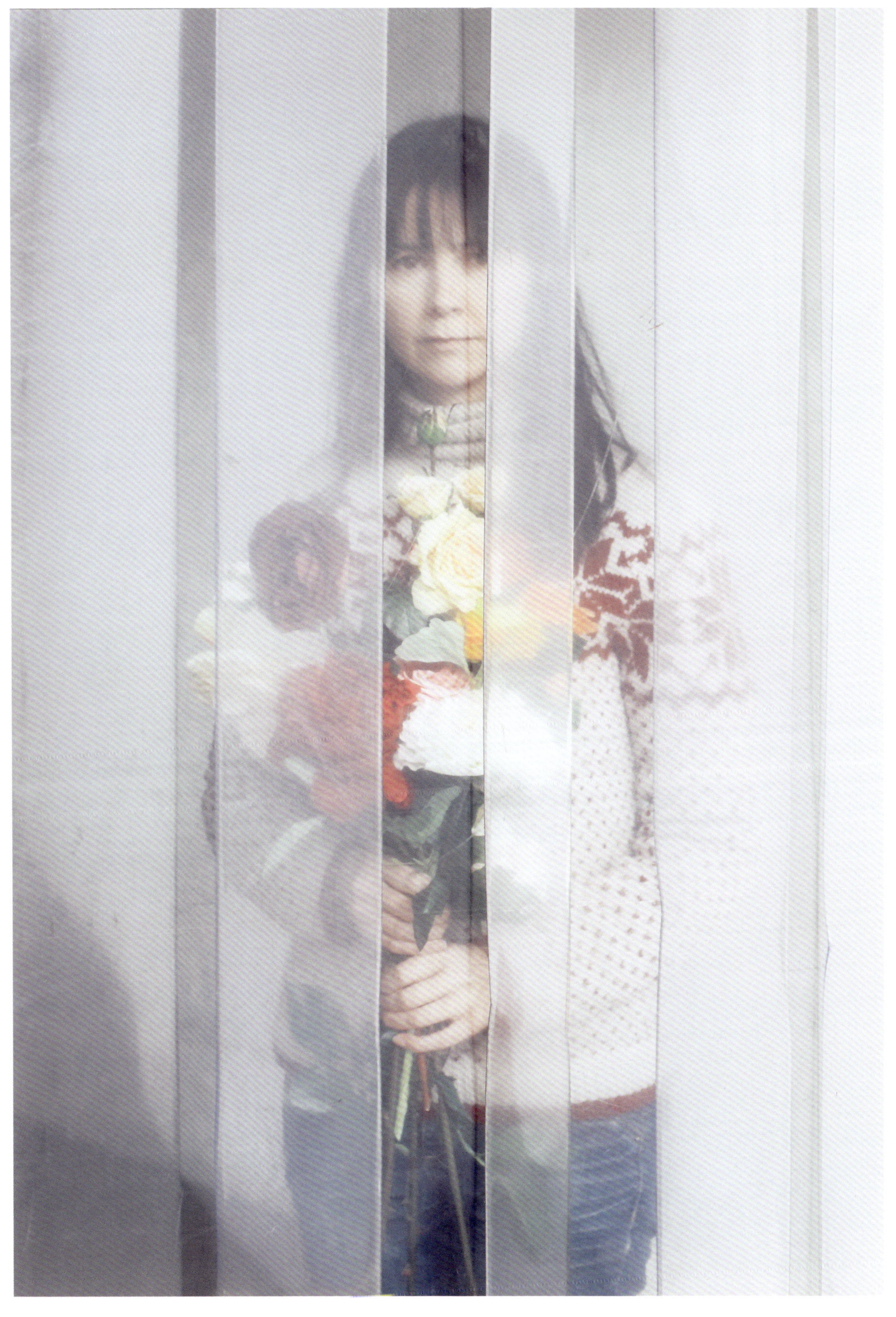

ROBIN FRIEND
GILLIAN WEARING
FROM THE SERIES SANCTUARY: BRITAIN'S ARTISTS AND THEIR STUDIOS
MARCH 2011

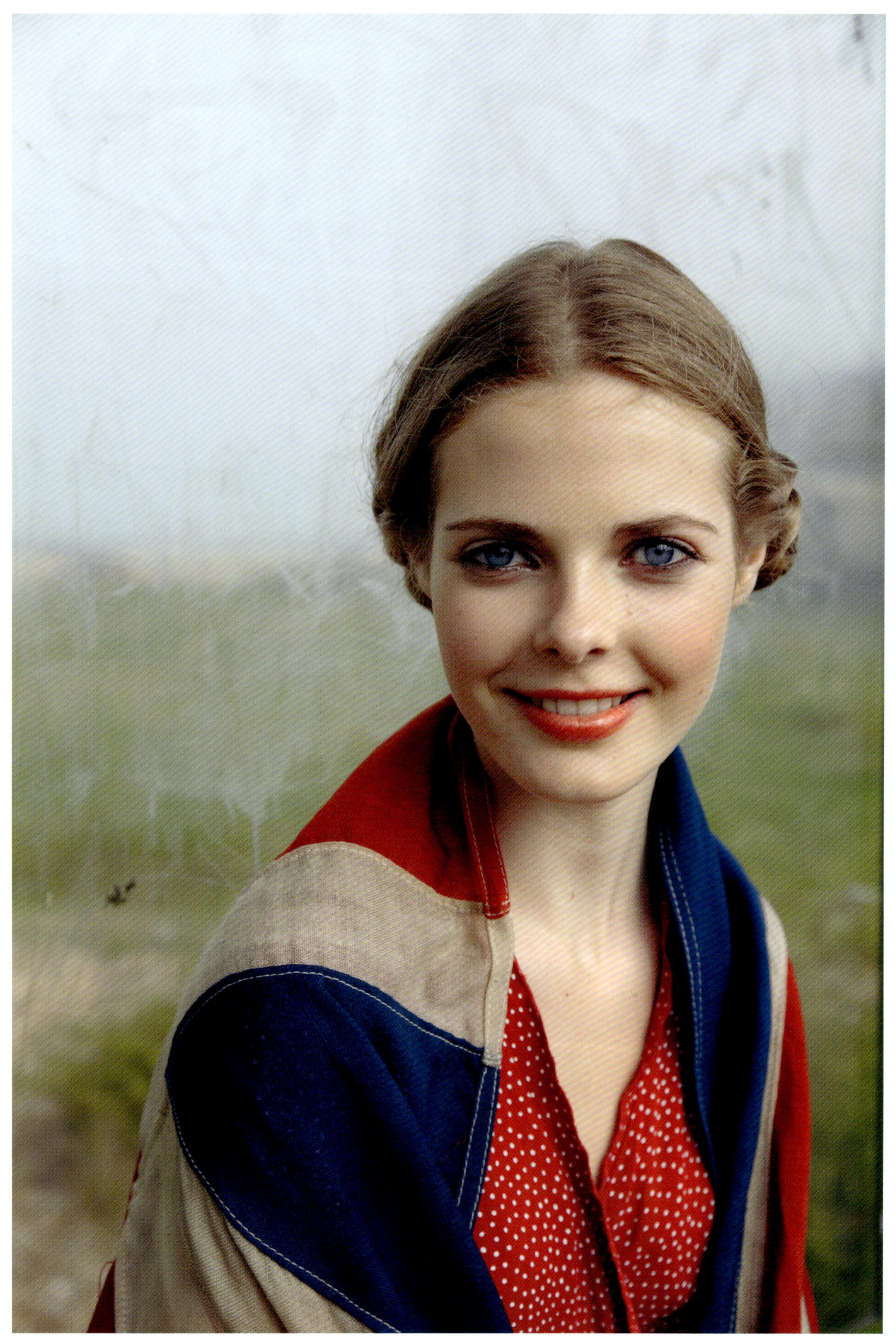

WENDY CARRIG
SOPHIE
FROM THE SERIES *BEAUTIFUL & WILD*
JULY 2011

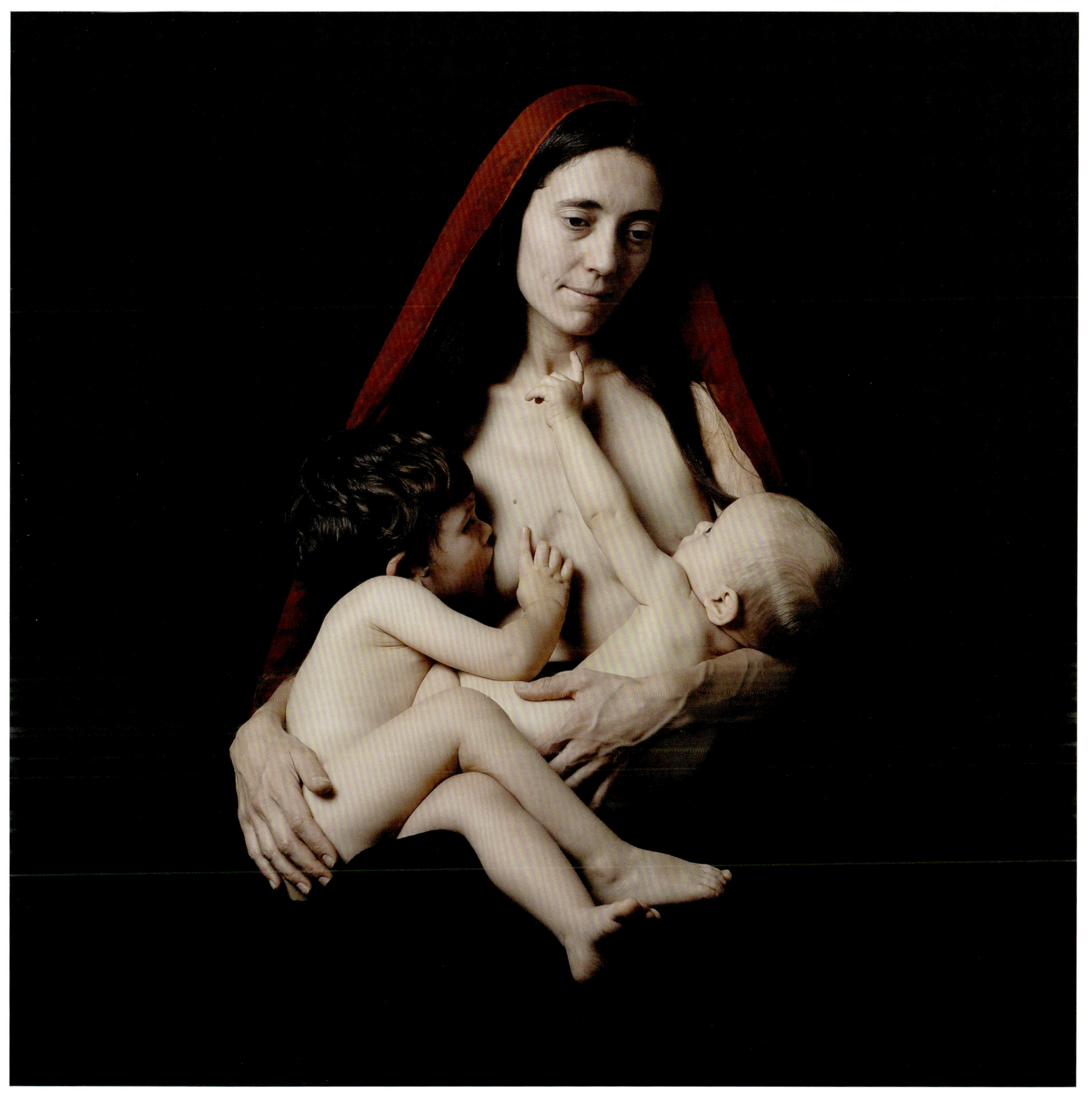

GEORGES PACHECO
AMÉLIE, XAVIER AND IRÉNÉE
FROM THE SERIES *AMALTHÉE*
APRIL 2012

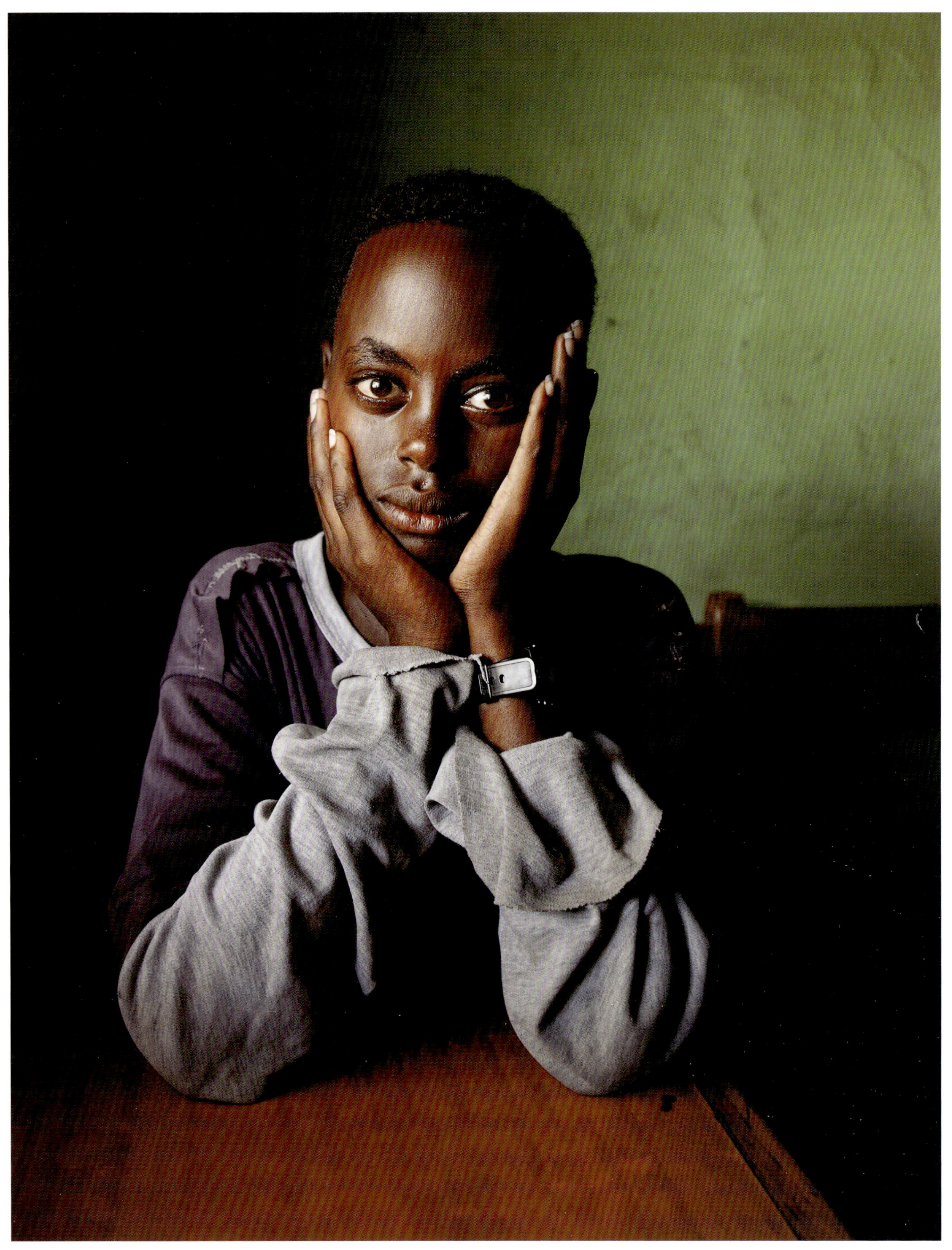

DAVID GRAHAM
FOOD FOR THOUGHT
NOVEMBER 2011

56

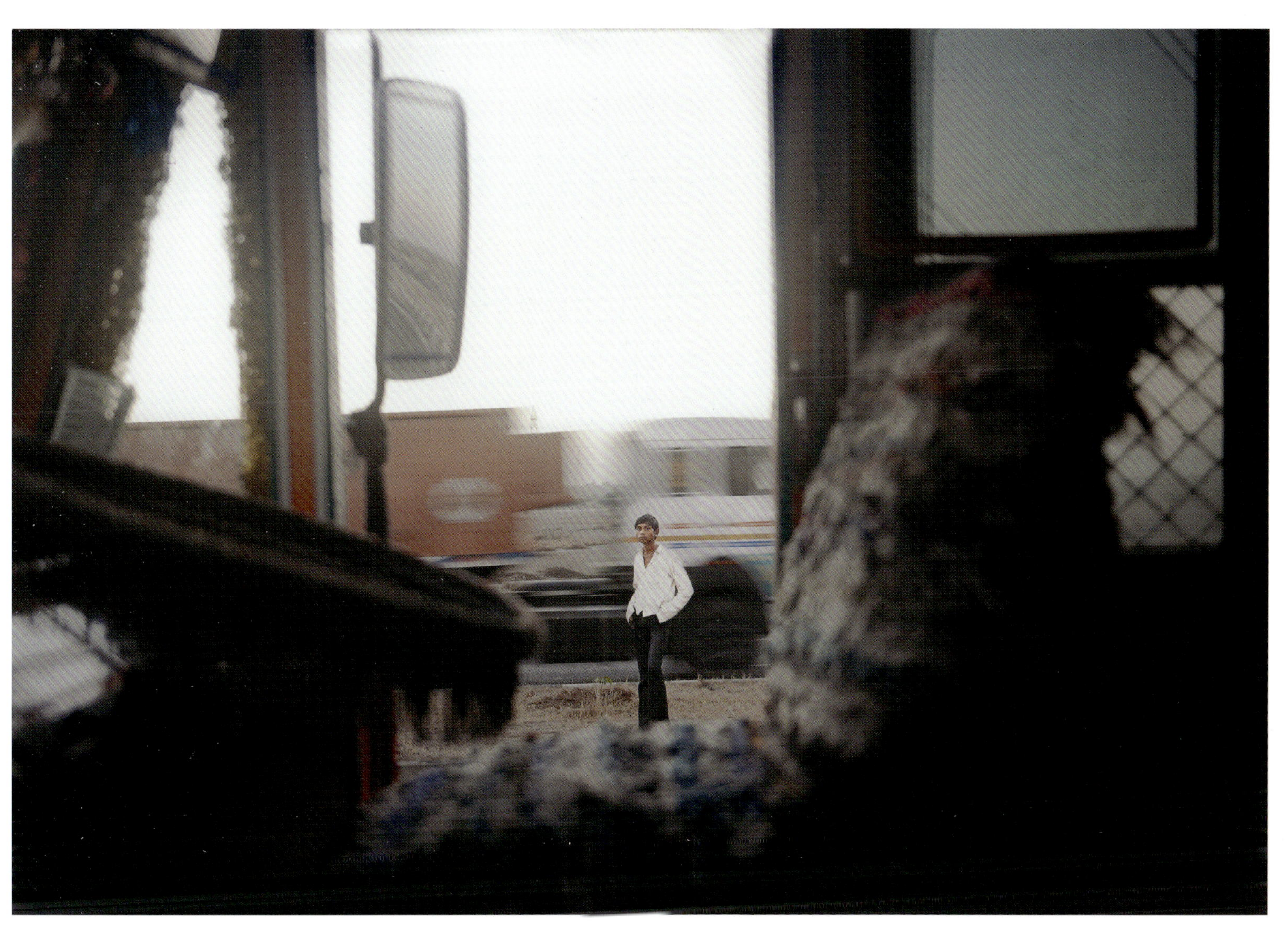

DARRAN REES
GUJARAT 1
DECEMBER 2011

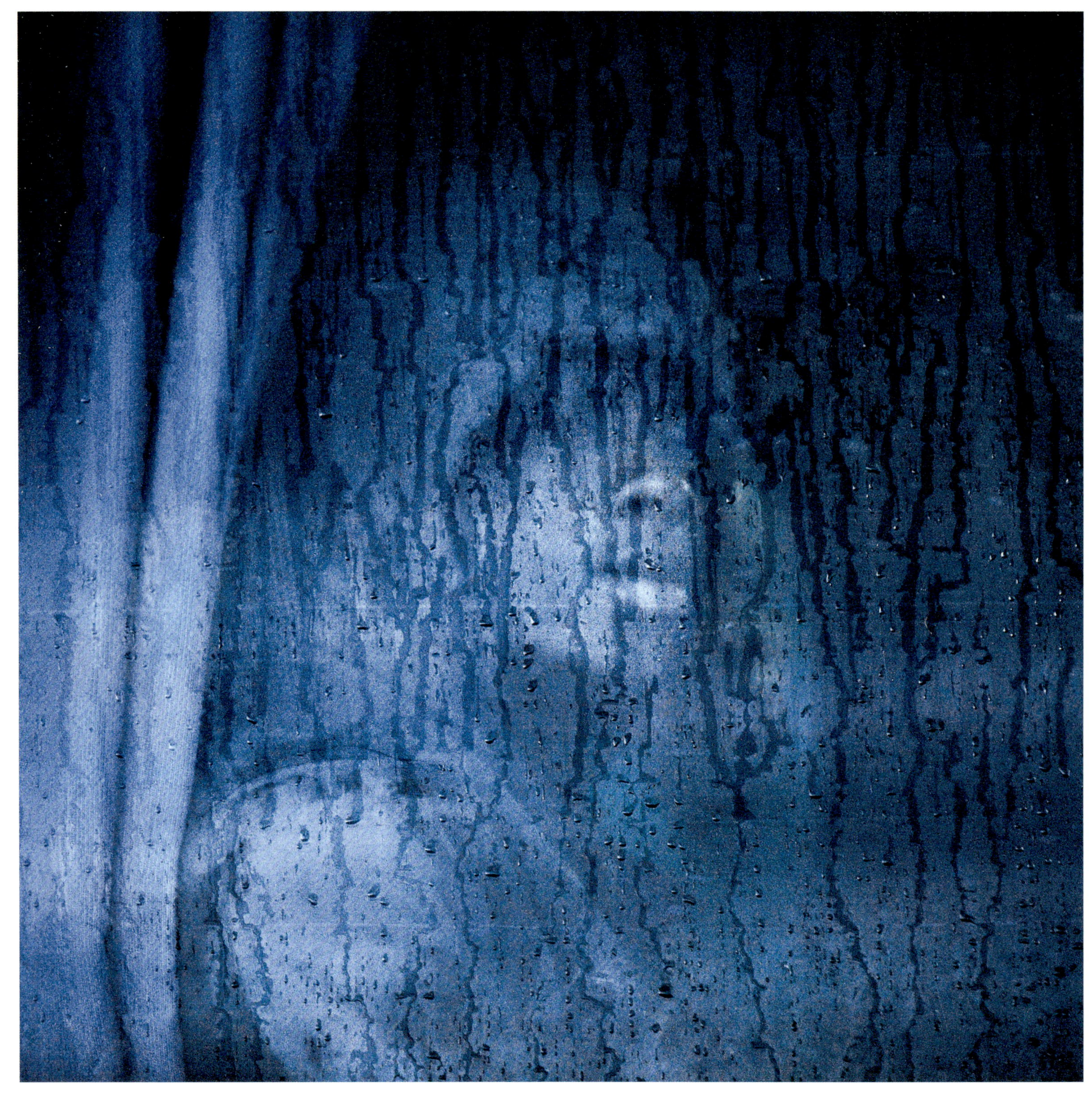

ANTOINE DE RAS
DISPLACED MIGRANT WORKER FROM LIBYA #1
FROM THE SERIES *TRAPPED IN TRANSIT*
MARCH 2011

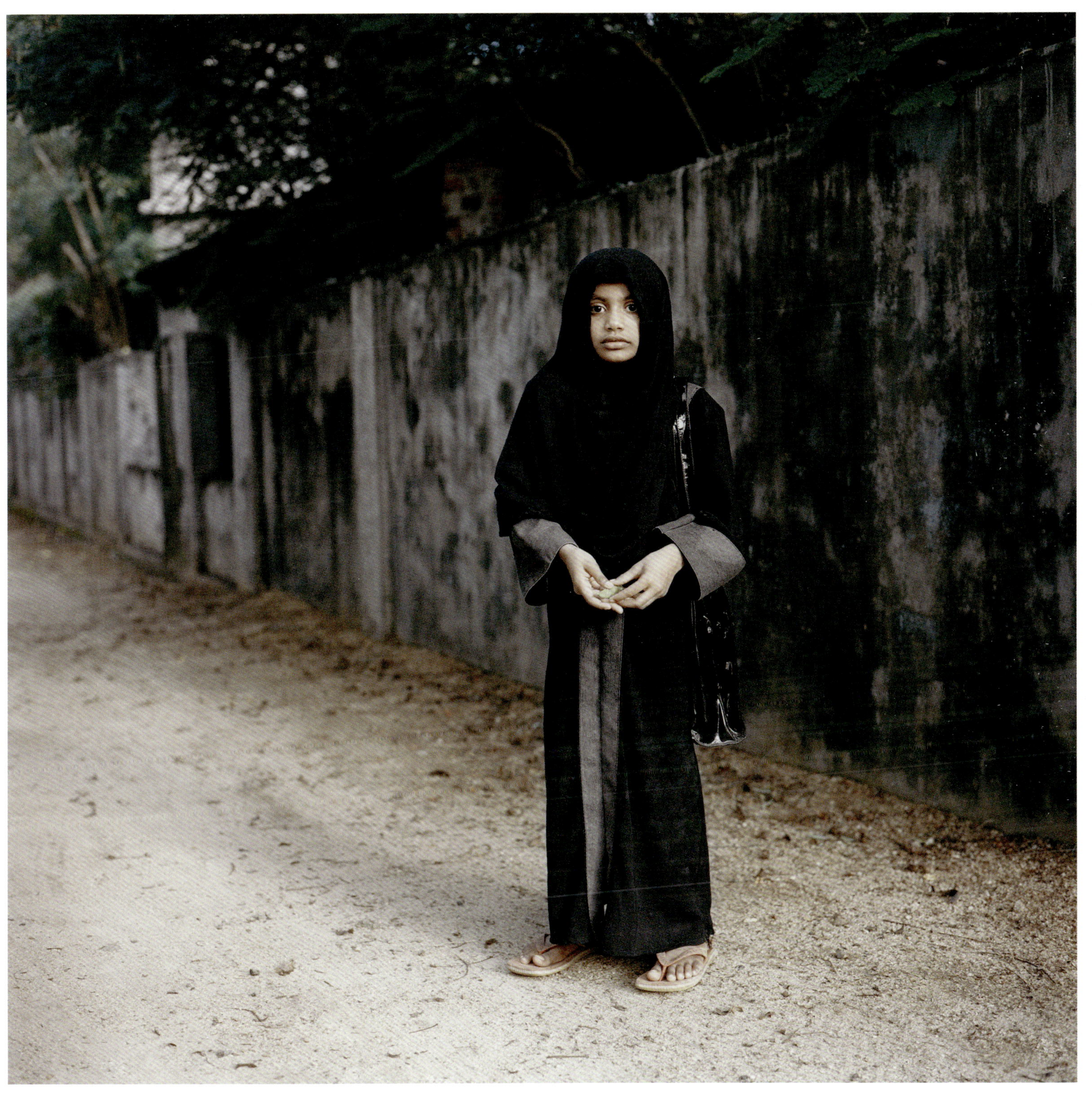

PAULA HOLTZ
FATHIMA
FEBRUARY 2011

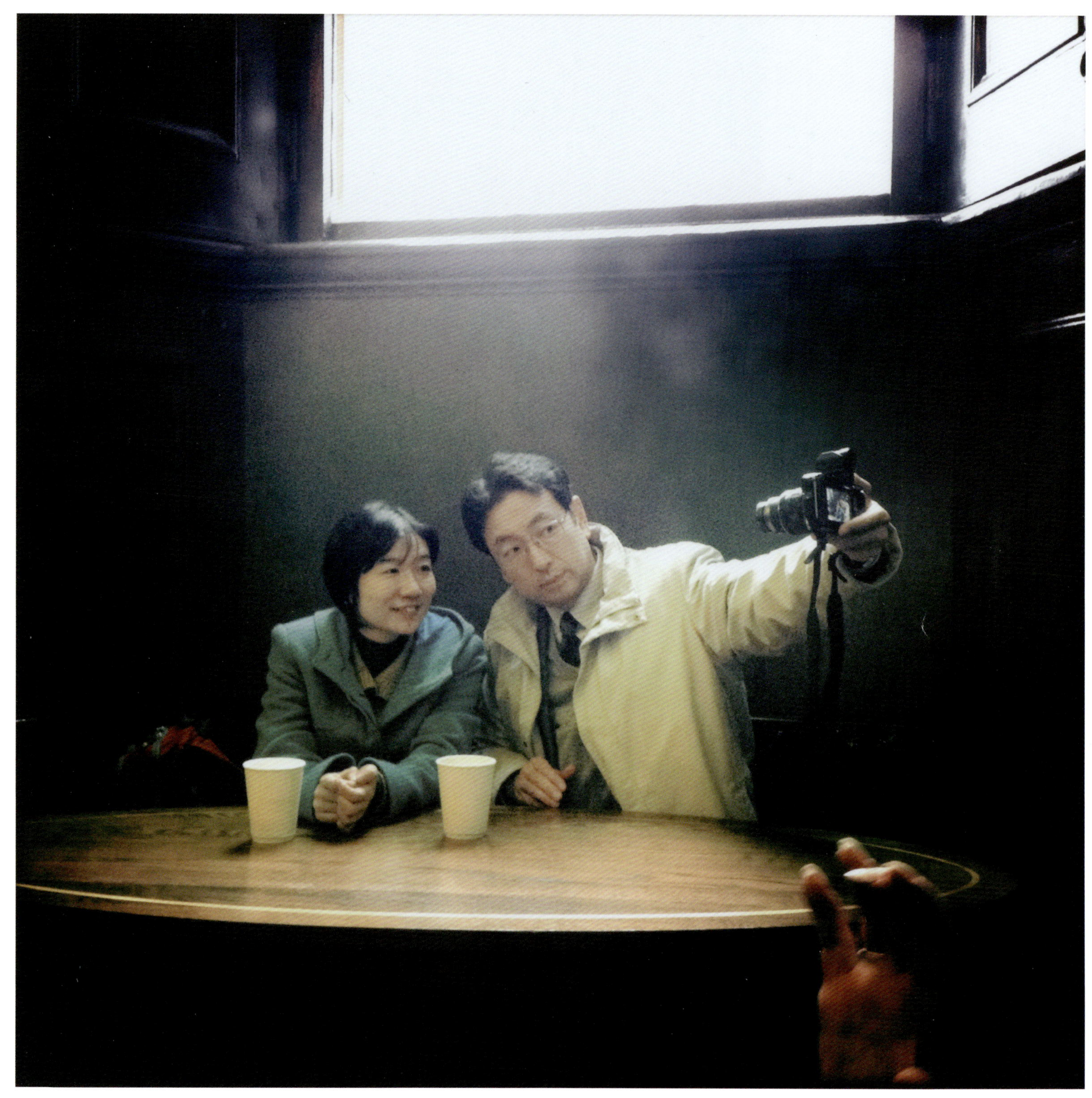

NATHAN ROBERTS
TOURISTS AT THE NATIONAL GALLERY CAFÉ, LONDON (IPHONE)
MARCH 2012

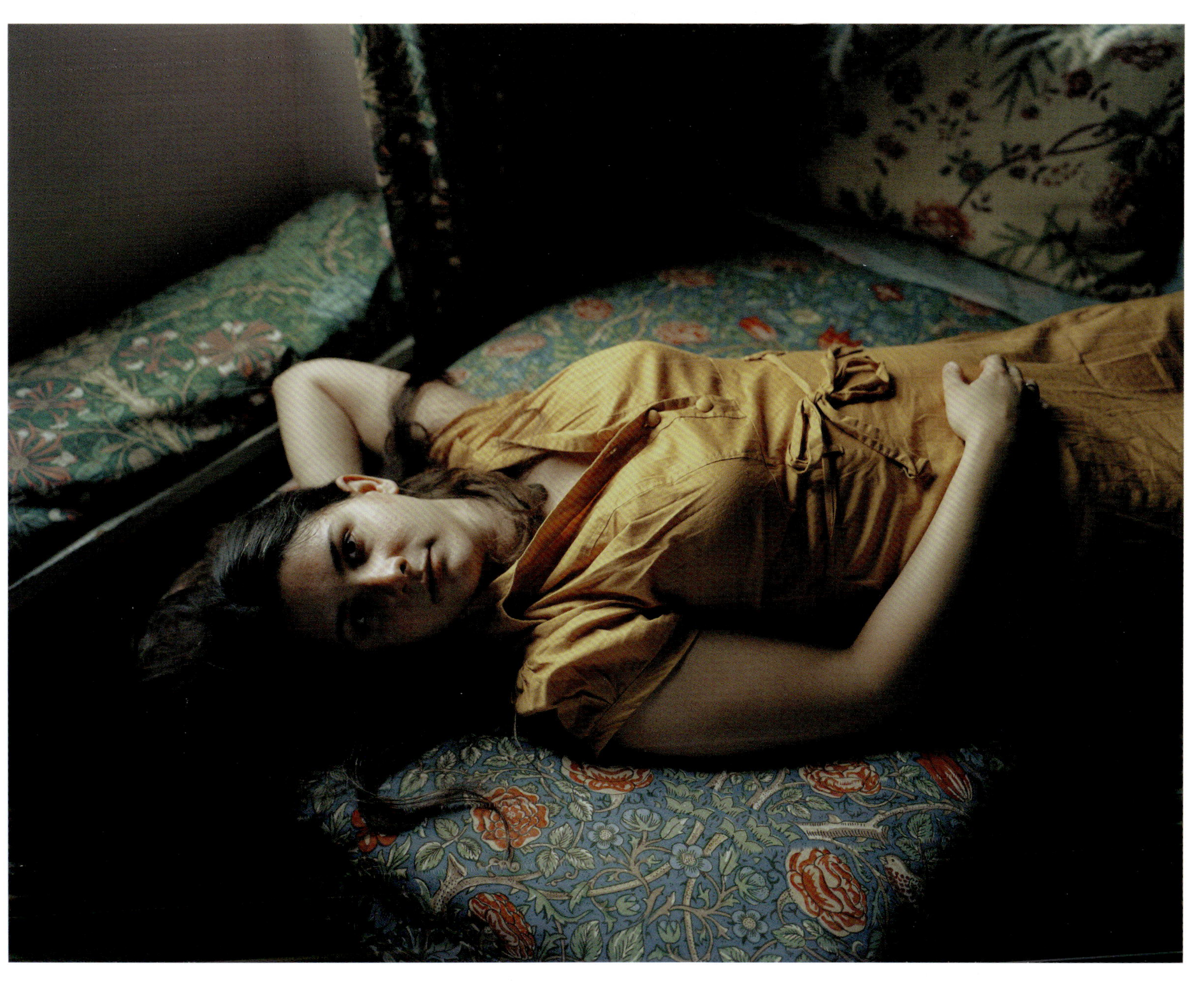

HERMAN NICHOLSON
UNTITLED (VIRGINIA AT EMERY WALKER HOUSE)
FROM THE SERIES *STAND GUARD OVER THE SOLITUDE OF THE OTHER*
JUNE 2012

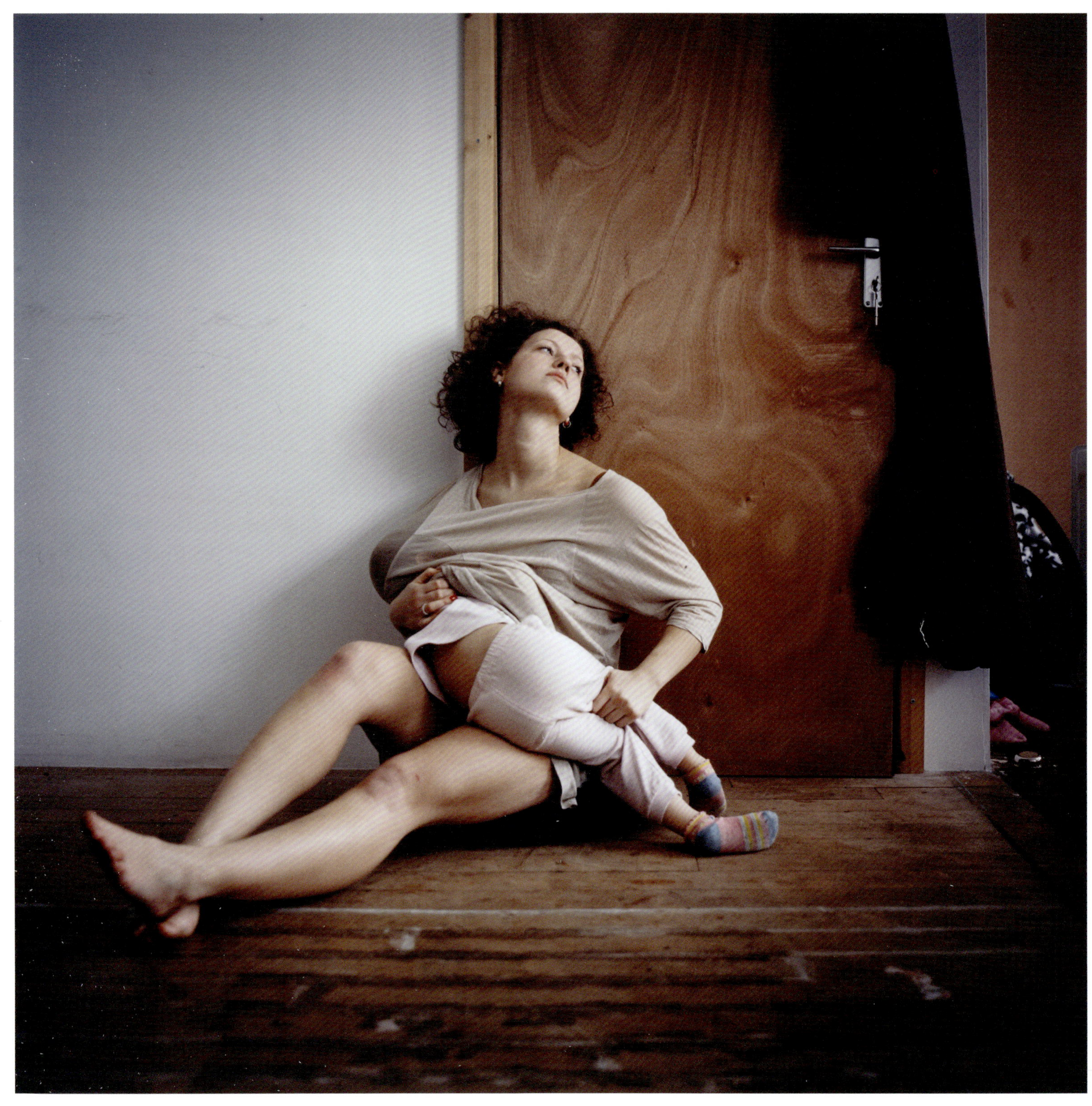

DAEWOONG KIM
SILENCE WITHIN
DECEMBER 2011

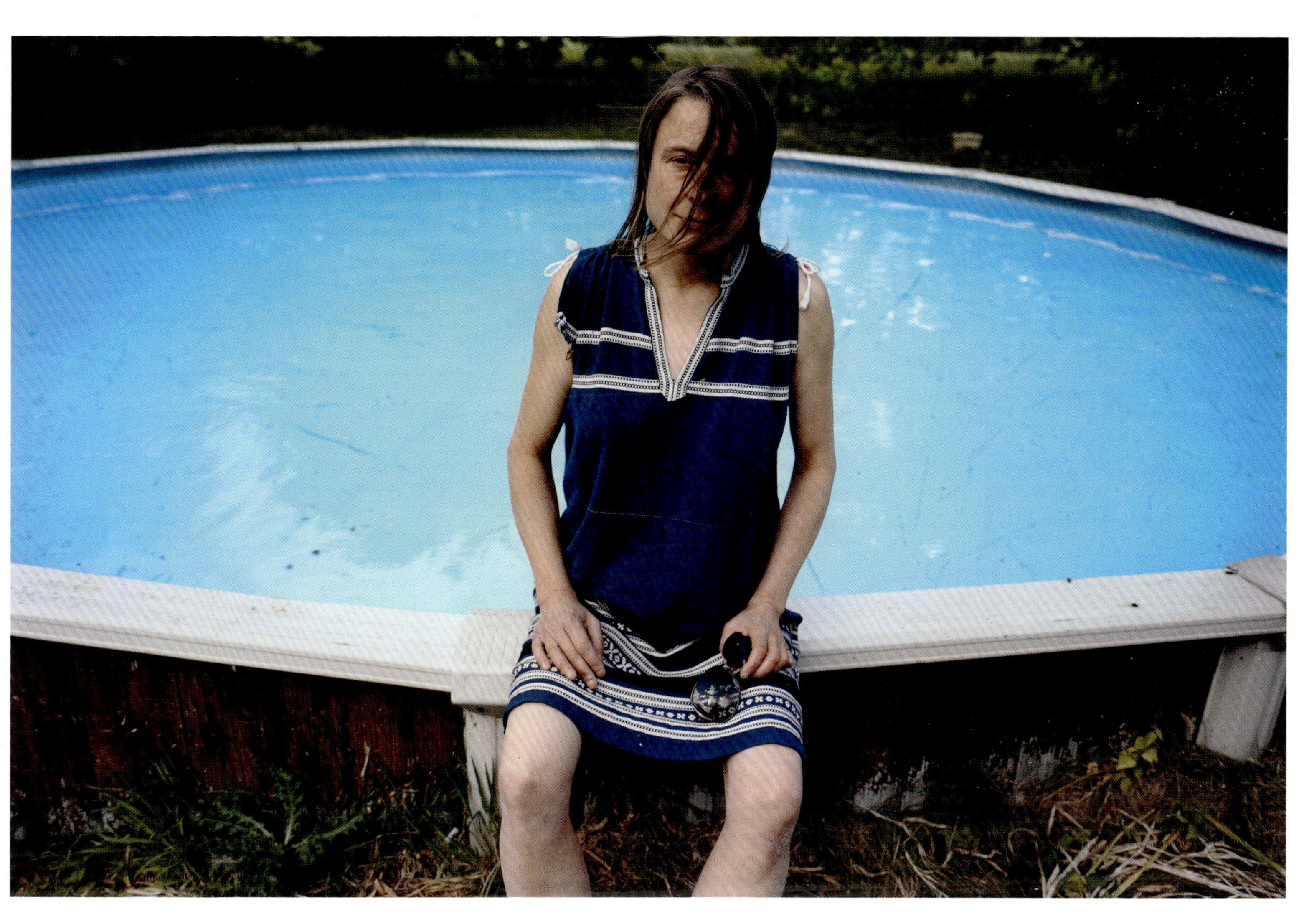

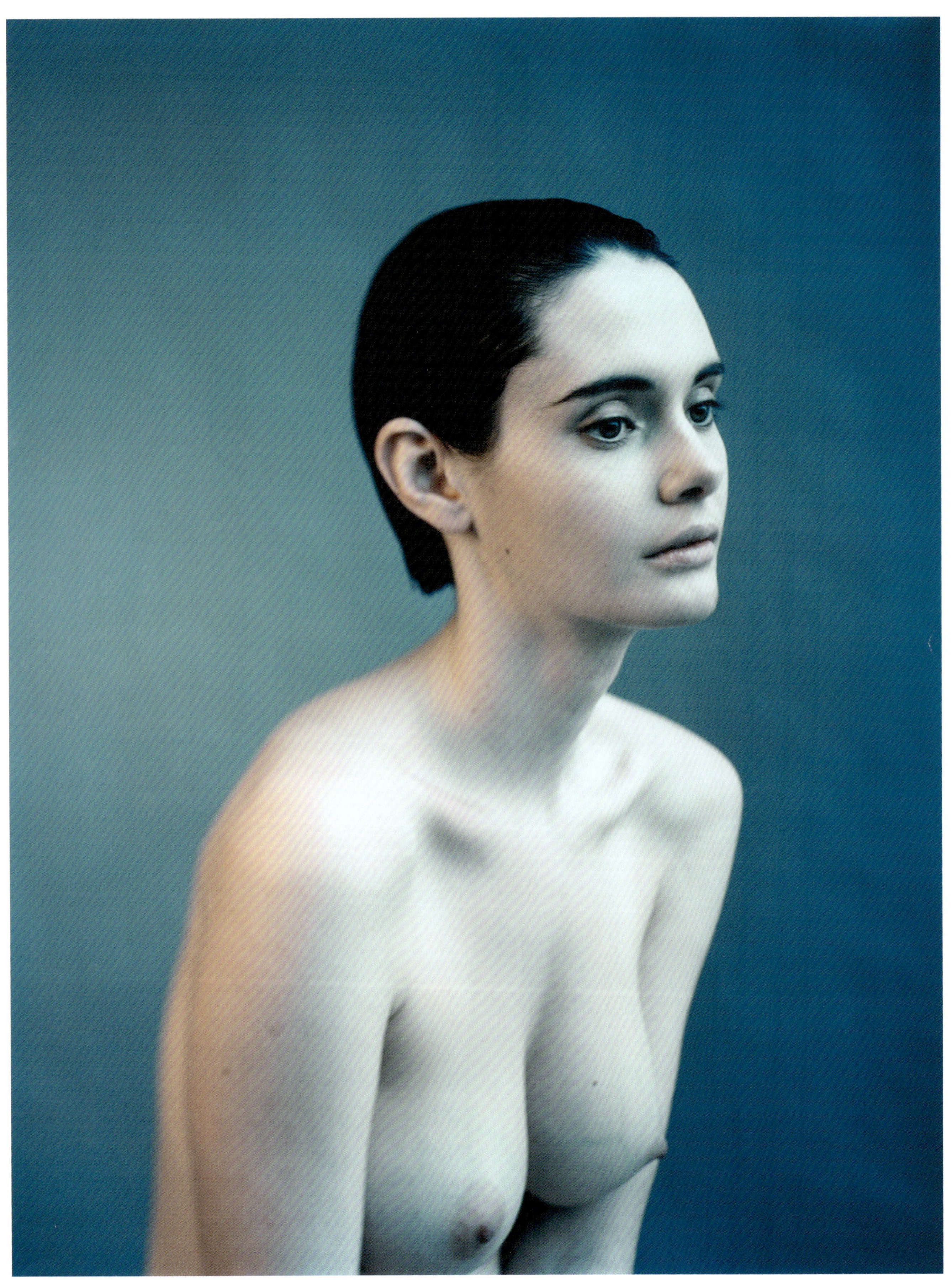

KAMIL SZKOPIK
JENNY
JANUARY 2012

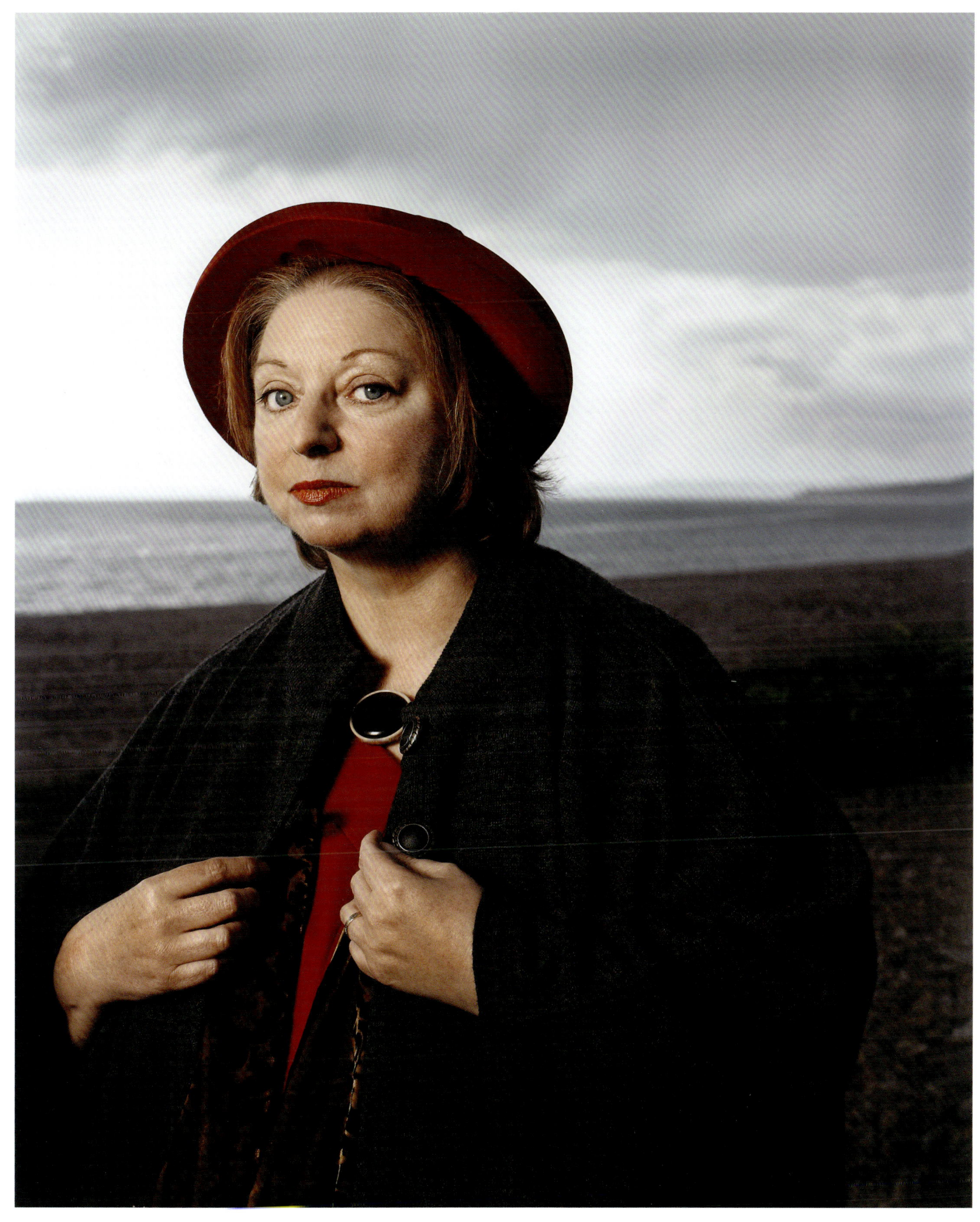

MICHAEL BIRT
HILARY MANTEL, CBE
APRIL 2012

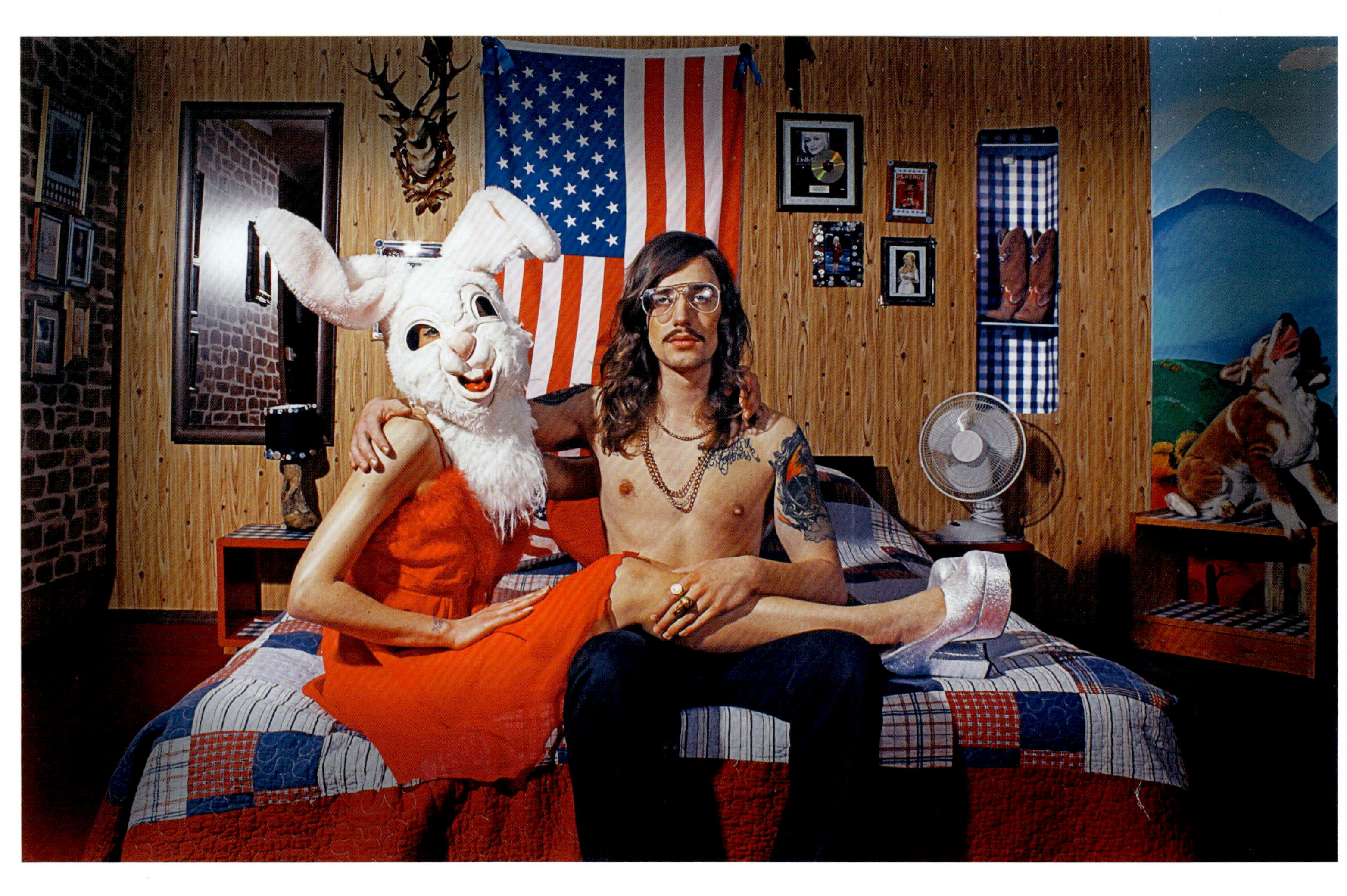

NADIA LEE COHEN
AMERICAN NIGHTMARE
FEBRUARY 2012

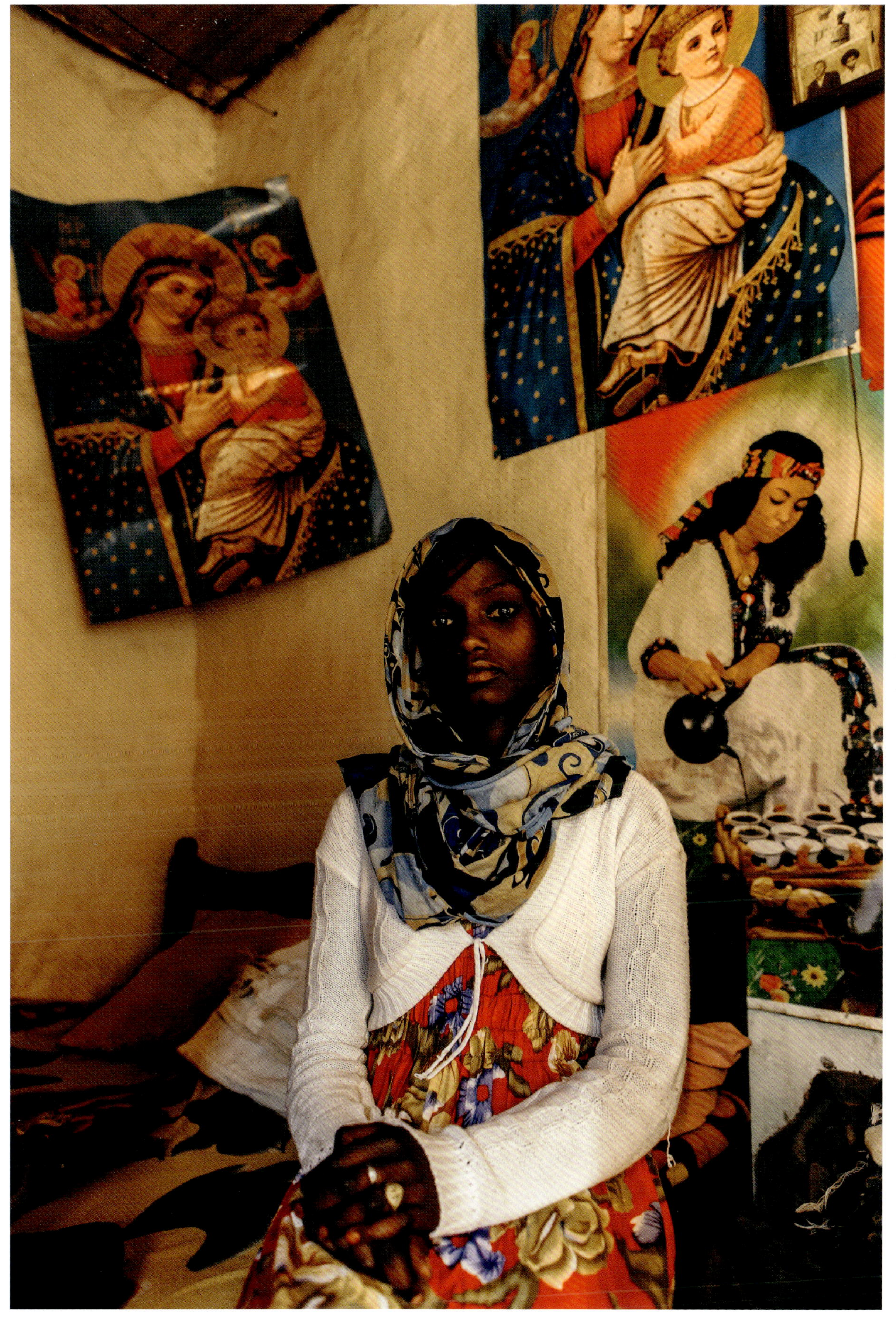

DAVID BRUNETTI
BREHANE
FROM THE SERIES *(UN)SAFE HOMES*
JULY 2011

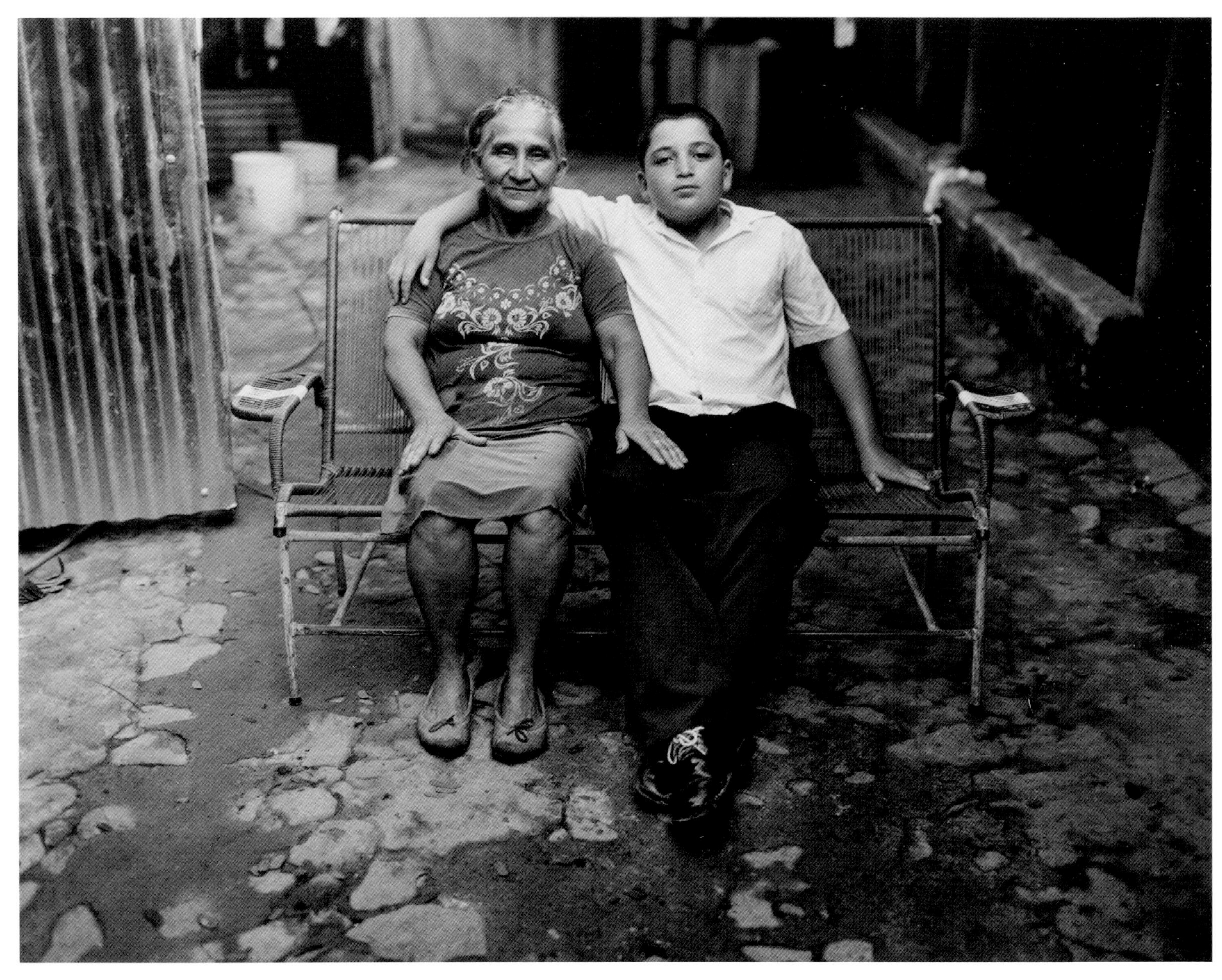

SARAH BOOKER
ROSA AND ADONEY, CHALATENANGO, EL SALVADOR
APRIL 2012

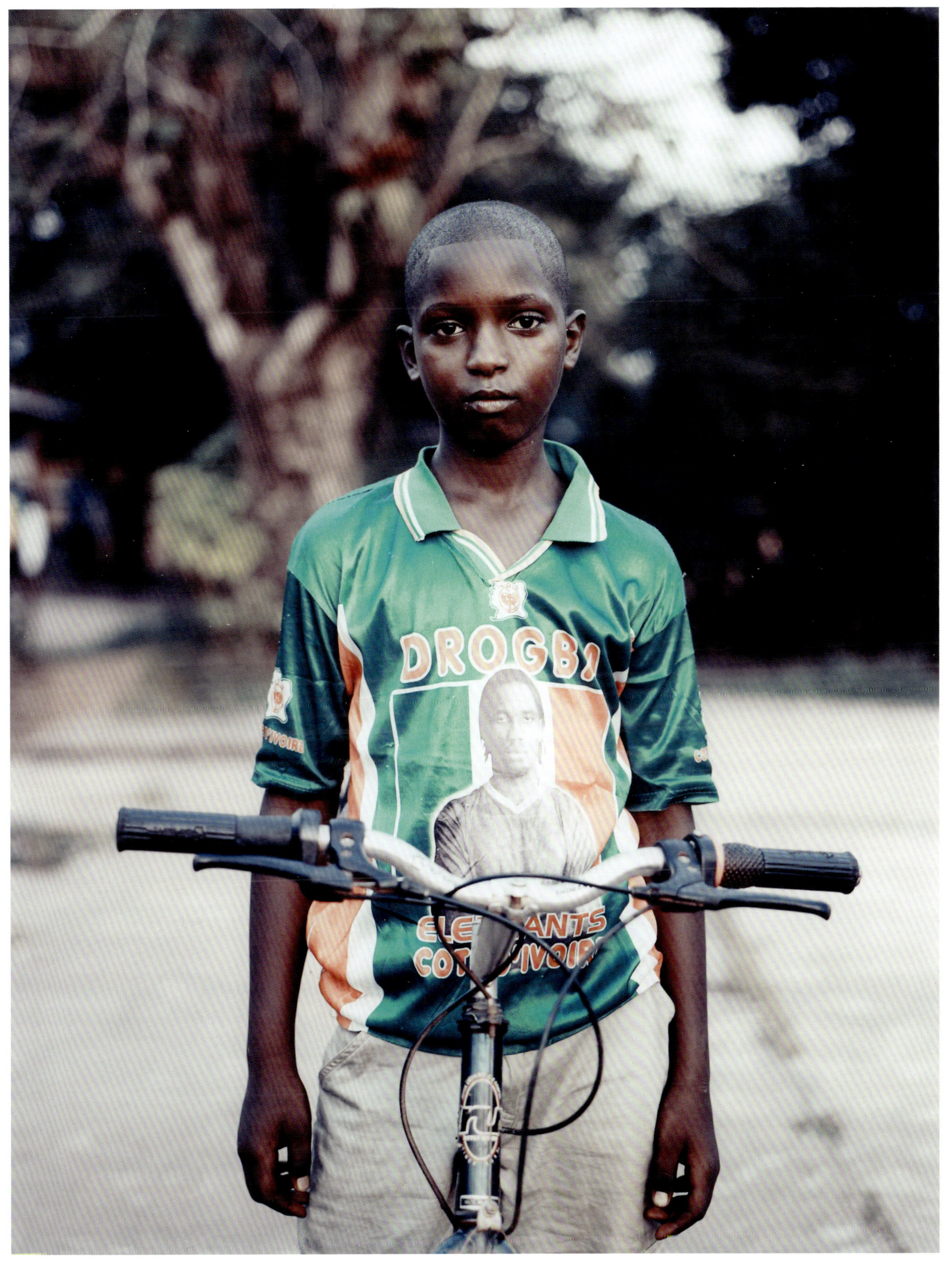

ALEXANDER KENNEY
KENEMA KIDS #08
FROM A SERIES OF PORTRAITS FOR LSTM & UNICEF, KENEMA, SIERRA LEONE
DECEMBER 2011

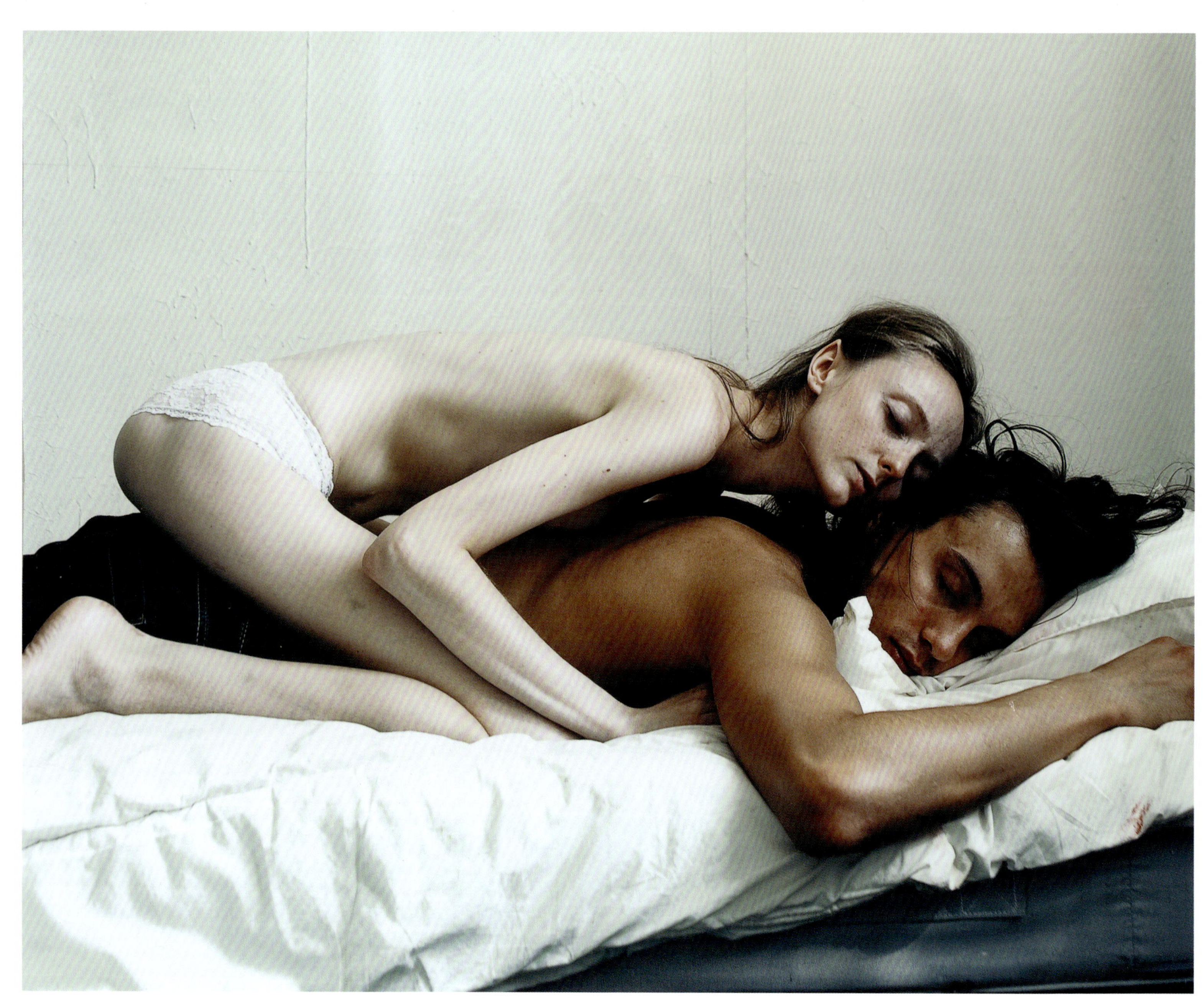

ELIZABETH HAUST
SILENCE
JULY 2011

CAROLYN COWAN
HRAFEN IX
FROM THE SERIES IN MEMORY OF A HORSE
JANUARY 2012

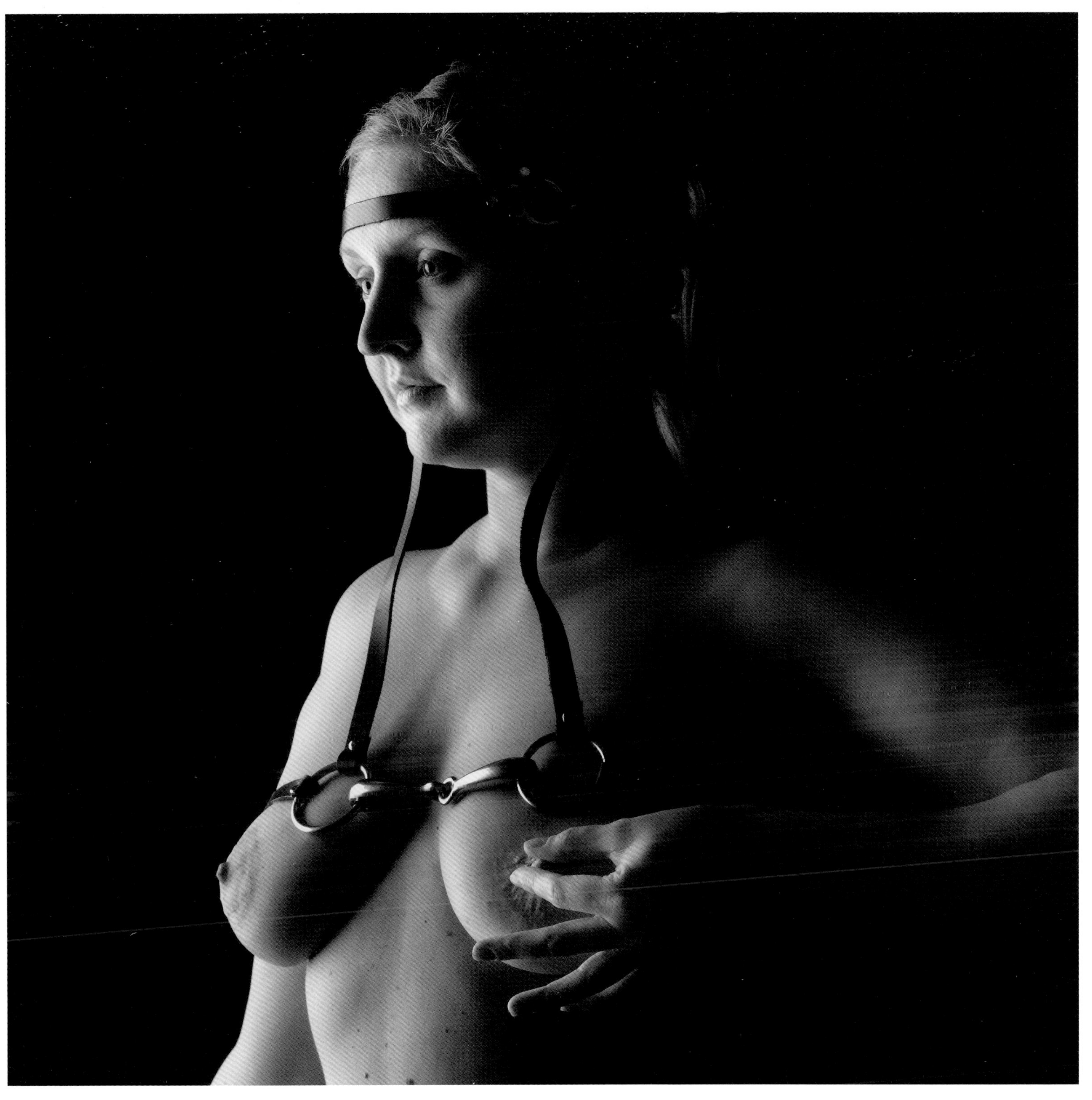

71

LIST OF EXHIBITORS